GREAT EVENTS
IN THE LIFE OF
CRAZY HORSE

Leads decoys in attack on Fort Kearny, December, 1866

arns his name, Crazy Horse, because brave deeds in battle, about 1859

Leads his warriors in battle against General Custer, June, 1876

Is made a chief of the Sioux, spring, 1876

THE STORY OF
Crazy Horse

"*Look!*" *he cried. "Man Afraid*
has failed—and here they come."

THE STORY OF
Crazy Horse

By
ENID LAMONTE MEADOWCROFT

Illustrated by WILLIAM REUSSWIG

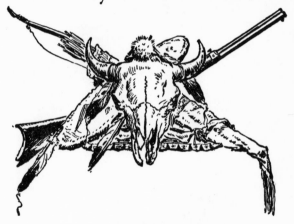

PUBLISHERS Grosset & Dunlap NEW YORK

PRINTED IN THE UNITED STATES OF AMERICA

LIBRARY OF CONGRESS CATALOG CARD NO. 54-5860

For
Manda Beaman
With Love

Contents

[*vii*]

THE STORY OF
Crazy Horse

He dived into the water

CHAPTER ONE

The Mysterious Messenger

IT WAS August—the month which the Indians called the Moon When the Cherries Turn Black. Soon the sun would begin his long walk from the east where the white man's country lay, beyond the wide Missouri River.

But now a few pale stars still shone over the great circle of tepees which had been set up near the Niobrara River. And all was quiet in the peaceful Indian village.

It was too quiet to please the Oglala boy, Curly, who would someday be called by his father's name—Crazy Horse. He lay wide awake on his bed of buffalo robes, waiting impatiently for daybreak. Waiting and listening.

Not far away he could hear his father snoring peacefully. From the other side of the tepee came the steady breathing of his mother and of Bright Star, his older sister. Close beside him, his younger brother, Little Hawk, murmured in his sleep.

Curly propped himself on his elbow and looked hopefully toward the entrance of the tepee. Only a thin streak of gray light showed under the flap which covered the opening. With a little sigh, Curly lay down again, still listening.

Blackbirds were waking and twittering in the rushes along the river. A horse tied outside one of the tepees whinnied softly. There was an answering whinny from one of the horses in the big herd on the hill. Then, at last, from the far side of the camp came the voice of the old camp crier.

"Co-o, co-o," called the crier as he started slowly around the big circle. "Get up, people. Co-o, co-o! Get up!"

Curly was out of bed almost before the first words had left the crier's mouth. He lifted the flap of the tepee and stepped outside. The sun was now up and it was a beautiful day. With a whoop of joy, Curly ran to the river to wash himself.

Quickly he unfastened the strip of rawhide which held up his breechcloth. He tossed the

[4]

breechcloth aside and dived into the water. It was cold and he came up spluttering. Many boys were now running toward the river. Curly called to one of them.

"I'll race you across to the other bank, He Dog."

He Dog laughed. "I could beat you with both hands tied," he cried, jumping into the water.

They struck out together for the opposite shore. He Dog reached it first. He watched with a grin as Curly came out of the water.

"I told you I'd win," he said. "You're still pretty small, Curly, for a boy who is nine snows old."

"I'll grow," Curly replied, shaking the water from his hair. "Some day I'll beat you. Just wait and—"

"Look!" He Dog broke in. "Here come Lone Bear and Little Big Man."

Curly glanced over his shoulder. Two more boys were swimming across the river. For some time all four splashed about, trying to duck one another and playing tricks in the water. Then they swam back across the river. Shivering, they stood on the high rocky bank, planning what they would do that morning.

[5]

He Dog had promised that he would take part in an arrow-throwing game, but the others decided to go hunting.

"We'll start as soon as we've eaten," Little Big Man said, beating his arms against his copper-colored body. "And we'll meet by the red rock under the crooked pine tree."

"With our horses?" Curly asked.

Little Big Man nodded and picked up his breechcloth, which he had left under a bush. He put it on. The other boys dressed, too. Then each one set out for his home.

By this time everyone in the village was awake. The sun shone brightly on the feathered spears and painted war shields which had been set on stands outside each warrior's tepee. Smoke rose slowly from scores of cooking fires.

Men were already sharpening arrows, testing bows, or standing about in little groups, talking. Women chattered together as they shook out sleeping robes or scraped buffalo skins which were pegged to the ground. Girls called back and forth while they gathered wood and brought water from the river. Naked little children romped underfoot. And bright-eyed papooses in cradle-boards swung

[6]

gently from the branches of the nearest trees.

Curly's mother stood beside the entrance of their tepee, brushing Bright Star's black hair with a porcupine tail.

"There is hot meat in the pot for you," she told Curly as the boy came up, breathless from running.

"And don't eat it all," Bright Star commanded, wincing as her mother's brush struck a snarl.

Curly chuckled and peered into the big iron pot.

"There's enough here for the whole Oglala tribe!" he exclaimed. "Umm, it smells good!"

He filled a large horn spoon with rich broth and buffalo meat. Picking a piece of meat from the broth with his fingers, he stuffed it into his mouth just as his father stepped from the tepee.

"Curly!" said his father in surprise. "Have you forgotten *Wakan Tanka?*"

Curly's face flushed a coppery red. He swallowed hard.

"I'm sorry," he said. "Please forgive me, great *Wakan Tanka*."

Carefully he offered the spoon full of food to *Wakan Tanka,* the Great Spirit, holding it

[7]

toward the sky, the earth, and the four directions.

His father smiled. "Now you may eat your fill," he said. "But remember always, my son, that it is *Wakan Tanka* who put us on this good earth and who gives us everything we need."

"I will remember," Curly promised soberly. He held out the spoon. "Will you have food, my father?"

"Later," replied Crazy Horse. "There is something else now that I must do."

He started toward the big council tepee which stood in the center of the circle. Curly watched him proudly.

Crazy Horse was the holy man of the tribe. The Oglalas believed that he could see what lay behind the moon, and the people asked his help whenever they were worried or in trouble.

"Even the chiefs come to my father for advice," Curly thought happily as he filled his mouth again with meat. "But *I* don't ever want to be a holy man. I want to be a great warrior like Hump or—"

He stepped back suddenly as Little Hawk darted past him, chasing one of their dogs.

Some of the broth from the big horn spoon slopped out on the ground. Curly drank the rest quickly and set the spoon inside the pot. Then he went into the tepee.

At the back of the tepee, just opposite the entrance, was a neat pile of cases called parfleches. They were made of buffalo hide and painted with bright designs. Curly opened one of these parfleches and took out a knife in a rawhide sheath. He stuck it in his belt. Then he closed the parfleche and reached for his bow and quiver of arrows, which hung from a tepee pole near his bed.

Dumping the arrows out on his sleeping robe, he counted them. There were five blunt, little-boy arrows and there were two with good iron points which his father's friend, Hump, had made for him. Curly stuck them back into his quiver and looked up to see Bright Star standing beside him.

"I know something you don't know," she said, tossing her black braids over her shoulders.

Curly grinned. "What girls know isn't worth any more than a wind in the treetops," he teased.

"This is," Bright Star told him quickly.

[9]

"It's important. Last night after you went to sleep, Chief Smoke brought a stranger here to talk to Father. And I heard him say he was a messenger from the—"

"Bright Star!" Her mother's voice came from outside the tepee. "I sent you in to get the scrapers so that we can work on the buffalo skins—not to spend all the morning talking to Curly."

Bright Star made a face. "I'll have to tell you the rest later," she said to her brother. Then she found two scrapers and hurried outdoors.

Curly watched her go, wondering what it was that she had overheard. Messengers often came into the camp from the Brulés or the Minniconjous or other friendly tribes. And girls were funny creatures, always trying to make little things seem big. He was glad he was a boy. He slung his quiver over his shoulder and picked up a halter made of braided buffalo hair. A moment later he was running toward the hill where the horses were grazing.

The herd was a large one, for the Oglalas moved their camp several times a year and each family needed a number of horses. Curly found his spotted pony with no trouble. She stood quietly while he put on the halter.

He grabbed her mane and swung himself to her back. Waving an arm at one of the older boys who was guarding the herd, he rode off toward the red rock by the crooked pine tree.

Lone Bear was already waiting at the meeting place and Little Big Man soon came along, carrying a rawhide rope. Then all three started off together into the woods.

[*11*]

CHAPTER TWO

"I'd Rather Be Dead!"

THE BOYS rode through the woods until they were some distance from the village. Then they tied their ponies to three small ash trees and went ahead on foot, keeping a sharp eye out for animal tracks or other signs of game.

Suddenly a rabbit hopped out from behind a bush. In an instant Curly had fitted a sharp arrow to his bow. He let the arrow fly and the rabbit toppled over, dead.

With a pleased smile, Curly picked it up and pulled out the arrow. Then, tucking the rabbit's head under his rawhide belt, he went on with the dead animal hanging at his side.

Soon Lone Bear shot a squirrel. Curly tried for another rabbit, but missed. Then Little Big Man found some deer tracks. The boys

[*12*]

squatted on their heels to examine them. Lone Bear thought the tracks were old, but Curly disagreed.

"You can tell by the way the dew lies on them that they were made this morning," Curly said, straightening up. "I think a doe made them. Let's see where she went."

They followed the tracks along a stream and around some chokeberry bushes. Suddenly Little Big Man, who was in the lead, held up his hand and motioned to the others to be quiet. He pointed ahead to a large brown fawn nibbling at some grass in a small open space. Lone Bear quietly reached for an arrow.

"Don't shoot her," Little Big Man whispered. "Let's catch her the way the men catch wild horses, and then we'll tame her." He uncoiled his rope, which had a loop in one end. "Now, Curly," he whispered, "give her the call."

Curly raised his fingers to his lips and made a little cry which Hump had taught him. It sounded like a buck calling a doe. The fawn raised her head. Curly called again and she moved a few steps in his direction. Then she stood still, bewildered.

[*13*]

At that instant, Little Big Man threw his rope. The loop settled around the fawn's neck.

With a frightened scream, the fawn leaped into the air, almost jerking him from his feet.

"Grab the rope!" he shouted.

Curly and Lone Bear both caught hold of the rope. Together the three boys managed to pull the struggling animal over to a tree. Lone Bear tied the end of the rope around the trunk. Panting heavily, the fawn stood still. Then she leaped again. The rope jerked her back.

"She'll wear herself out soon," Little Big Man said. "When she's quiet we can drag her home and make a pen for her."

He sat down on the ground to wait. The others stood beside him, watching the trembling fawn. She stared at them, her brown eyes filled with terror. Suddenly she sprang forward again. But she could not escape.

For some reason Curly was beginning to feel strangely uneasy. Tears flooded his eyes as he watched the fawn fight so frantically to get free. All at once he could stand it no longer. Yanking his knife from his belt, he ran up and quickly cut the noose around the fawn's neck.

"Now go!" he cried, slapping the young deer on the flank. "Go, I say! Go!"

The fawn bounded away and Little Big Man jumped up.

"What's the matter with you, Curly?" he shouted angrily. "Haven't you any sense? What did you do that for?"

"I don't know," Curly replied, ducking his head quickly so that his friends could not see his face. "She—she was trying so hard to get free. And it would be awful to be shut up in a pen. I'd—I'd rather be dead!"

"But the fawn wasn't all yours," Lone Bear protested hotly. "It was ours, too. You had no right to let it go. You ought to give us something, Curly, to make up for it."

"You can have my rabbit," Curly replied in a muffled voice. And, wiping his eyes hastily, he ran to get the rabbit, which he had dropped near the chokeberry bushes. When he returned, both Lone Bear and Little Big Man reached for the rabbit at the same moment. Then Lone Bear laughed.

"It would look funny if we each went home with half a rabbit," he told Little Big Man. "Anyway, I'm hungry. Let's all cook it right now, and eat it."

Little Big Man agreed, and the fawn was quickly forgotten as he skinned the rabbit while Lone Bear and Curly made a fire. Soon the boys were roasting hunks of juicy meat over the coals.

The sun had passed the middle of the sky by the time they had finished eating. Little Big Man picked up his knife, which was lying beside him in the grass, and plunged it into the earth several times to clean it.

[16]

"I wish I had a good sharp white-man knife like that," Lone Bear said. "Where did you get it?"

"My father got it for me at the trading fort on the white-man road," Little Big Man replied. "He got a red blanket, too, and some tobacco. All for three buffalo hides. But that was before the soldiers came to the trading fort."

"Soldiers?" Curly looked up curiously.

"Yes, white-man soldiers in blue coats," said Little Big Man. "They moved into Fort Laramie and the traders moved out to another place down the road. That's what my father told me."

"Did he see the Blue Coats?" Lone Bear asked.

Little Big Man nodded. "They are walking soldiers with thunder-sticks," he said. "But there aren't very many of them."

He slipped his knife into its rawhide case and, getting to his feet, he began to stamp out the fire. Lone Bear stood up to help him. But Curly sat still, with his knees hunched under his chin, thinking about the blue-coated soldiers.

As a little boy he had often seen the fort

where the soldiers were staying. It was close
to the road which the white men had made
right through the Oglala hunting grounds.

Many times, when the Oglalas were camping near that road, Curly had watched long
lines of white-topped wagons which were traveling west. He had stared with wondering
eyes at the strange, pale-skinned people who
stopped now and then near the fort to rest,
and to cook their food. Once he had played
with a pale-skinned papoose and tasted some
sweet white sand which the papoose's mother
called "sugar."

But all that had happened when Curly was
quite small. Since then, Oglala warriors, like
the father of Little Big Man, had sometimes
gone to the fort to trade. But the whole tribe
had not been there for many moons.

"I'd like to see that fort again some day,"
Curly thought. "I'd like to see the Blue Coat
soldiers with their thunder-sticks and—" He
jumped as Lone Bear prodded him with his
foot.

"Come on, Curly," Lone Bear said. "We're
going home."

The boys picked up their bows. Slinging
their quivers over their shoulders, they ran

to get their ponies. Soon they were riding through the woods toward the village.

As they came in sight of it, they realized at once that something unusual was going on. All of the old people and the women and children were sitting around the huge council tepee in the center of the village. The sides of the tepee had been rolled up and the council lodge was filled with warriors.

They were seated in three circles, one within the other. Some of them seemed to be arguing. Others were laughing. And there was a great deal of noisy talking.

Sliding from their ponies, the boys turned them loose and hurried over to find out what was happening. Curly saw his mother sitting with Bright Star and Little Hawk at the edge of the crowd, and ran to squat down beside them.

"That man's gone," Bright Star said before Curly could speak.

"What man?" Curly asked breathlessly.

"That messenger I started to tell you about. He came from the white-man soldier fort to ask us all to a big council there. And there's going to be a feast and—"

"And presents," Little Hawk broke in, leaning across his mother. "Many presents from the white men. But some of the warriors don't want to go, so—"

"Shh!" said his mother sharply. "Hump is going to speak. Listen!"

Curly craned his neck to look at the tall warrior who now stood before the others. Hump's long black braids were wrapped in fur, and a single eagle feather was fastened upright in his hair. As he folded his white buffalo robe proudly across his chest, Curly felt sure that there was no finer warrior in all the world. He listened intently to Hump's words.

"My friends," Hump began, in a deep, quiet voice, "I do not understand these white men. We have always been their friends. It is true that a few of our wild young men have sometimes made a little trouble for travelers on the white-man road. But there has never been a war between us. Yet the whites have brought their soldiers into our country.

"Now they ask us to a council to talk about something they call a treaty. And they offer us presents. I do not know what they want in return for these presents. But I think we must go to their fort and find out."

"And I say that we should have nothing to do with the white men," cried a young warrior named Red Cloud. "Their thunder-sticks have frightened away many of our buffalo. Their breath spreads sickness among us. Yet each day more white men push into our country. And more will come—and more! Let us drive them out before it is too late."

"*Hou*," cried a few of the warriors in agreement. And even one or two of the women cried, "*Hou!*"

Then Chief Smoke stood up.

[*21*]

"Our brave young warrior, Red Cloud, speaks with a wild tongue," he said slowly. "He tells you that more white men will come. Many more cannot come. I am an old man and the whites have been passing through our country since I was a boy. They all travel toward the place where the sun sleeps and few of them return. Soon there will be none left in their land to the east. So let us talk no more about driving them away. They are our friends. Let us keep peace with them and go to their council."

"Hou," cried many of the people all together, in loud, strong voices. *"Hoppo!* Let us go!"

And so the matter was settled. Smoke announced that the journey to Fort Laramie would begin the following day. The meeting broke up, and the people started for their tepees, all talking about the white-man council and the soldiers and the presents.

That night Curly was so excited that he could hardly get to sleep. And when he did, he had a strange dream. He dreamed that he was a fawn with a long rope around his neck. Two white men were dragging him along a wide trail. Suddenly one of them turned and ran at him with Little Big Man's knife in his hand, and the dream ended.

When he woke next morning, however, it was still fresh in his mind. He started to tell his mother about it, but she was too busy taking down the tepee to listen to him. And in the excitement of moving, he forgot it.

All through the village, women called back and forth as they took down tepees and folded buffalo robes and packed parfleches. Some of the boys drove the horses down from the hill where they were grazing.

As soon as the morning meat was eaten, the shafts of the travois were harnessed to the pack horses and to some of the dogs. Tepee poles and coverings, as well as household articles such as parfleches and cooking pots, were placed on some of the travois. Then the old people and the small children climbed onto others.

Everyone else was on horseback by this time. Each family took its place in a long line headed by Chief Smoke. And long before the sun was halfway to the middle of the sky, the Oglalas were on their way.

Five days later they set up their village on Laramie Creek, just south of the fort.

CHAPTER THREE

The White Men's Promise

―――――――――――――――――――――――――

"WAGON-BOXES! *Hoka hey! Hoka hey!*"
Curly, Lone Bear, and He Dog shouted like
warriors as they galloped down the dusty road
to meet a train of six covered wagons. When
they had almost reached the first wagon, they
swerved off the road and lined up to watch
them all roll by.

"These wagon-boxes aren't as big as the
ones we saw this morning," Curly said. "Look,
there's a paleface squaw with a little papoose."

"Two papooses," He Dog corrected him.
"And a girl with hair as bright as fire. What's
that boy in the next wagon-box holding?"

"It looks like a baby wildcat, only it's
white," Lone Bear replied. "Here come some
more of their smelly spotted buffalo. Hold
your noses!"

He backed his pony away from the road as

a small herd of brown-and-white cows plodded after the last wagon. A freckle-faced boy on a thin black horse was keeping the cows on the road. Curly waved his arm at the white boy in a friendly greeting.

But the white boy, like most other west-bound travelers, had heard many frightening tales about Indians. He could not tell the difference between tribes that were hostile to white men and tribes that were not. To him, all Indians were alike and they were all bad. So he simply stared hard at the three young Oglalas and rode past them, yelling sharply at one of his cows.

"What's the matter with him?" He Dog exclaimed. "He acts as if he were angry with us."

"Hou," agreed Curly. "Many of them act
that way—but I don't know why." He glanced
at the sun. "It's almost time for the Blue Coats
to make their walking lines," he added. "Let's
go over to the fort and watch them."

Wheeling his horse around, he galloped
across a wide, dusty plain toward Fort Laramie. Lone Bear and He Dog followed him,
whooping and kicking their moccasined heels
against the sides of their ponies.

Three sleeps had passed since the Oglalas
had set up their camp on Laramie Creek, just
south of the Platte River. The Brulé Indians,
too, were encamped near the creek, and the
Minniconjous, and four other tribes which belonged to one great nation, the Teton Sioux.
Their painted tepees spread far out over the
broad plains, and their grazing horse herds
looked like dark clouds of grasshoppers on the
distant hills.

Not all the Indians who had been invited
to the council had arrived yet. But those who
had come were having a fine time—racing
their horses, playing ball games, feasting,
dancing, and visiting their friends.

Curly had twice visited the Brulé village down the river, for his mother was a Brulé and he had many Brulé relations. Now, as he galloped toward the fort with Lone Bear and He Dog, he saw some of his relatives standing with the other Indians who had gathered near the big white adobe building. They were watching the Blue Coats, who had already begun to make their walking lines.

The soldiers carried thunder-sticks over their right shoulders. Walking briskly, they kept in step, and all looked straight ahead. Suddenly their leader shouted at them and they all spun around quickly and walked the other way. Soon the leader shouted again, and once more the soldiers spun around.

Lone Bear grinned. "It makes me laugh every time I see them do that," he said to Curly. "Do you think they fight that way, too? All together, and waiting for a leader to give them orders?"

"I don't know," Curly replied. As he watched the soldiers retrace their steps, he was thinking of the way the Oglala warriors fought. They had no leader to command them. Every warrior fought as he pleased, and tried to count coup on his enemy before he attacked him. A man had to be very brave to count coup. He must go straight up to his enemy and hit him with his hand, or with a special coup stick. Counting coup took more courage than killing.

"When I'm a warrior, I'll count more coups than anyone else," Curly told himself. "I'll count coup on the Crow Indians when they attack us, or when we go to steal their horses. And I'll count coup on the Pawnees and on—"

There was a sudden burst of noise. Curly jumped and He Dog laughed aloud. The leader of the soldiers had shouted again, and the Blue Coats had fired their thunder-sticks into the air.

"I'll bet if one of the white-man wagon guns spoke, you would jump higher than that, Curly," said He Dog. He looked hopefully at the two small cannon which stood near the fort. "I wish they'd shoot one off so we could hear it speak. Did you know the Crows were coming to the council?"

"The Crows!" Curly could hardly believe his ears. "But they're our enemies!"

"They're coming just the same," He Dog told him, "and so are the Snakes. But my father said that the chiefs of all the tribes have agreed that there'll be no fighting among us. Look, Curly, the Blue Coats are going to make their thunder-sticks speak again."

Curly nodded and Lone Bear patted his pony reassuringly, for she had shied after the first burst of gunfire. The boys waited until the soldiers had finished their drill. Then they rode over to the little log trading houses which were not far from the fort.

There two warriors were pounding out iron arrowheads on the blacksmiths' anvils. Red Cloud stood laughing and talking with one of the traders—a jolly fat man named Jim Bordeaux. Near them several Cheyenne Indians were loafing in the sun.

The whole Cheyenne tribe had just arrived that morning. Several days later the Snakes reached the great encampment. And then the Crows came riding over the hills from the north.

There was no fighting between the tribes, for the chiefs had kept their word. But a problem had come up which worried everybody. The horses—thousands of them—had already eaten all the grass for miles around the fort!

"Soon there will be no grass left here.

Those horses will starve if we don't find another meeting place quickly," said Colonel Mitchell, the white-man chief who was in charge of the council. And he decided that everyone should move to the rich grassy lands near Horse Creek, some thirty miles east of the fort.

So it was that on a warm September morning a strange procession set out down the white-man road. Two hundred and seventy blue-coated soldiers led the way. Several carriages filled with white men followed the soldiers. Big covered wagons, loaded with food and supplies, rumbled along behind the carriages. And then came the Indians—more than ten thousand of them—gaily decked in paint and beads and feathers.

Dogs barked. Babies cried. Women shouted at the horses which were pulling the travois, or called to children who had stopped to play along the way. Young men and small boys whooped loudly as they galloped up and down the long column, showing off how well they could ride. Yet the people of each village managed to stay together. And the following day everyone was comfortably settled in a great encampment on Horse Creek.

Two mornings later the first council meeting was held in a big lodge made of buffalo skins, which the women had built in the center of the encampment. Chiefs of each tribe filed proudly into the lodge to smoke the long, feathered pipe of peace with the white men.

They listened politely to Colonel Mitchell, as he explained why he had asked them to come.

Meanwhile, everyone else gathered around the lodge. It was a quiet crowd. But it was so vast that Curly, who was with his family on the outer edge, could not see or hear what was going on. Not until late that evening did he find out what had happened at the meeting.

He was lying on his sleeping robe, only half awake, when Hump, Smoke, and a Brulé chief named Little Thunder came into the tepee to talk with Crazy Horse. They seated themselves at the back, behind a small fire, and puffed on their pipes in silence for some time. Then old Smoke turned to Hump and Crazy Horse.

"It seems that the white chief, Mitchell, has been sent to us by the Great White Father who lives in a far-off place called Washington," he told them. "Mitchell talked loud and strong before us this morning and his words were put into our tongue by a man named Wyuse."

"What did he say?" asked Hump. "Did he speak about the treaty paper?"

Smoke nodded. "It is a paper full of promises," he said. "The whites want us to promise that no Indian will ever harm travelers on the white-man road which runs through our country. They want to build more forts along the road. And they want us to promise that there will be no more fighting among us."

[32]

"Peace among the tribes will be good," Crazy Horse said thoughtfully. "And what will the whites promise?"

"That they will be our friends forever," Little Thunder replied. "But we must touch the pen while our names are put on the treaty paper. Then we will be given the presents which the Great White Father has sent to us. And there will be more presents for us at Fort Laramie every summer for fifty years."

Curly pricked up his ears. Presents every summer for fifty years! He could hardly wait to tell Lone Bear and He Dog and Little Hawk and all the other boys. Truly, the Great White Father was a generous man!

"But how can I ever count coup on a Crow if there's to be no more fighting among the tribes?" Curly thought.

He was still wondering about this when he fell asleep. And he thought of it again on the day the chiefs and the white men met and signed the treaty. But he forgot it completely when a long wagon train, loaded with the presents from the Great White Father, rolled into the huge encampment. Everybody crowded around the wagons. And soon the presents were handed out.

[*33*]

Each chief who had touched the pen re-
ceived a splendid gold-trimmed general's uni-
form of blue, and a bright gilt sword. For the
other people there were hatchets and knives
and twists of tobacco, strings of brightly col-
ored beads and sacks of coffee and sugar.
There were yards and yards of red flannel and
blue calico, too, and gay blankets, and little
round mirrors, and papers of fine vermilion
powder to be used in making red paint. There
was something for everyone and everyone was
pleased with his gift.

Curly was given a little mirror, just like the
signal mirrors which the warriors wore on
rawhide strings around their necks. Early next
morning he stood on top of a low hill, proudly
flashing signals to Lone Bear, down in the
camp. But before long, Little Hawk came running up the hill.

"The council's all over," he said breathlessly, "and Smoke's given the word to move.
Mother wants you to come and take out the
top tepee pins."

So Curly ran home with the mirror bump-
ing up and down against his chest. When he
reached the tepee, he climbed up the center
pole and pulled out the wooden pins which

held the covering together at the top. Then he helped his mother and Bright Star fold it up and load it onto one of the horses.

Throughout the great encampment other Indians were also taking down tepees, rounding up horses, and packing travois. And before the sun had passed the middle of the sky, the tribes were starting off in all directions.

The Oglalas splashed across the shallow Platte River and headed north for the buffalo country. As they climbed a low hill beyond the Platte, Curly stopped beside his father and Hump, who had turned to look back. For a moment all three sat on their horses, gazing down at the white-man road. A column of soldiers was marching toward Fort Laramie.

"Will there be soldiers at the fort when we come next summer to get our presents?" Curly asked.

"Yes," replied Hump. "The treaty paper says that soldiers will always be there. Little Thunder told me so this morning."

Crazy Horse shook his head doubtfully. "That news makes my heart heavy," he said in his quiet voice. "As long as white soldiers remain in our country, trouble will be lurking behind every moon."

CHAPTER FOUR

Red Streak

CURLY pulled back on his bowstring with all his might and sent an arrow flying through the air. When it dropped to the ground, he looked up at Hump.

"That went farther than the last one," the tall warrior said encouragingly. "But not far enough for a boy who's eleven snows old. Perhaps your new bow is too strong, younger brother."

"No," Curly replied sturdily. "My arms are too weak. But I'll make them strong, Hump. I'll practice every day until I can send an arrow from here all the way to that aspen tree. Then will I be ready to hunt buffalo?"

Hump shook his head. "You won't be ready until you have a good horse," he said. "Your pony's getting too old to chase buffalo. Pick up your arrows now, and we'll go home."

Curly ran to gather up his arrows. As he put them into his quiver, he told himself that

Hump was right about the spotted pony. She wasn't fast enough for buffalo hunting. And his father had no other horse to give him.

"I must get a good horse," he thought. "Perhaps Hump will help me."

He hurried to overtake the warrior, who had already started for the village. As they walked along together, Curly waited hopefully for Hump to mention horses again. But Hump only said gravely, "Tomorrow, younger brother, I challenge you to fast all day."

Curly looked up at him quickly. He had known for several moons that some day Hump would offer him this challenge. Soon after the Oglalas' second trip to Fort Laramie to get presents, Curly, his father, and Hump had had a long talk. They had discussed what Curly would do when he was grown up.

"I'm going to be a warrior," Curly had said, standing very straight before the two men and trying to look tall and strong. "I want to be the bravest of all the Oglalas."

Hump's eyes twinkled. "And whom will you fight?" he asked. "Since we made peace with all the tribes at the Treaty Council, it seems we have no enemies."

"But no one can tell how long that peace will last," Crazy Horse said slowly. "Some day we may need warriors badly—"

"And I *want* to be a warrior," Curly insisted.

[*38*]

"Then I myself will train you," Hump had promised, with a little smile. "But the training will not be easy, younger brother. There will be many difficult things for you to learn besides how to fight.

"A good warrior must be able to run for a day and a night with only short rests. He must know how to blaze a trail through wild, trackless country. And he must be strong enough to go for two or three days at a stretch without food or water."

"All those things I will learn," Curly had promised soberly.

Now at last the time had come for him to begin learning to go without food and water. And he was glad.

"Tomorrow," he said to Hump, "I will not eat or drink all day."

The next morning Hump went early to Crazy Horse's tepee. He blackened Curly's face with charcoal as a sign that the boy was fasting, and sent him out to spend the day as he pleased.

As soon as Curly stepped from the tepee, Little Hawk, Lone Bear, and a horde of other boys gathered around him. Little Hawk tempted him with a spoonful of delicious-smelling stew. And Lone Bear stuck a piece of juicy buffalo steak on the tip of his white-man knife and held it under Curly's nose.

"Eat, Curly," he teased, while the others danced up and down, talking about food. "Eat."

"Tomorrow I'll eat," Curly said. And he walked away.

Most of that day he spent by himself, wandering over the hills and along the river, growing hungrier and thirstier every minute. When the sun had walked far down the western sky, Curly passed a patch of wild turnips and pulled one out of the ground. It looked crisp and juicy and his stomach was crying out for food. For a moment he stared at it longingly. Then he hurled it into the river and watched it float out of sight.

His throat was parched and his mouth was dry, yet he did not even wet his lips with river water. Trying to forget his hunger and thirst, he climbed a low hill and gazed across the plain.

An eagle floated lazily against the pale blue sky and a band of antelope grazed in the wide valley below him. Beyond the antelope, five buffalo were wallowing in a shallow, muddy

pool. And on the sand hills beyond the buffalo—

Curly squinted his eyes and stared hard. All
at once he turned, bounded down the hill, and
started for home on the run. Lack of food had
made him dizzy and he stumbled twice, falling
flat on the ground. But he picked himself up
and ran on through the deepening dusk.

It was late in September—the Moon When
the Buffalo Calves Grow Hair—and the air
was cool. In the village, fires glowed through
the skin walls of many tepees. When Curly
pushed aside the flap over the entrance to his
father's tepee, he found Hump seated with
the family, sharing their evening meat. Curly
dropped to the ground beside him.

"Wild horses!" he panted, as soon as he
could catch his breath. "There's a big herd of
them. More than I could count. On the sand
hills—between here and—Crow Butte."

Hump looked at him quickly. "You're
sure?" he asked. "You didn't dream it because
of your empty stomach?"

"No," Curly insisted, staring hungrily at
a turtleback plate filled with stew. "I saw
horses."

The smell of food and the long run home

[*41*]

had made him feel weak. Suddenly he was almost too tired to hold his head up. Stumbling to his feet, he threw himself down on his buffalo robes and fell asleep at once. He was still sleeping soundly when his mother shook him next morning.

"Get up, my son," she said, "and eat well. The men are going after those horses you saw yesterday, and Hump wants you to ride along with them."

Curly was up in an instant. He raced to the river to wash the charcoal from his face, wolfed down some morning meat, and ran to get his spotted pony.

It had been some time since the last horse hunt. And because of the promises made at the Treaty Council, the Oglalas had taken no horses from the Crows. Now, many people needed horses and all through the village men were getting ready for the chase. Each man supplied himself with a strong rope made of braided buffalo hide, and a long willow pole with a noose at one end.

Soon they all rode off toward the sand hills. Hump led the way, with Curly, on his pony, riding proudly beside him. When they reached the top of the hill from which Curly had seen the wild horses, they stopped. Curly scanned the hills quickly and sighed with relief. The horses were still in sight.

"There they are," he said, pointing them out to Hump.

Hump nodded and turned to give some instructions to the men. Quietly they began to ride around the herd, keeping behind the hills, and making a huge circle several miles wide. As soon as this circle was complete, the men at the south galloped toward the wild horses, yelling loudly. With tails and manes flying, the frightened animals bolted to the north. But there, more yelling men blocked their way.

Wherever the horses turned, their escape was cut off. Back and forth the hunters drove them, across the wide, grassy valley, trying to tire them out so that they would be easy to catch. At last, each man started after the horse he wanted to capture.

Hump rode hard on the flying heels of a beautiful young sorrel mare. Whipping up his spotted pony, Curly tried to stay close behind him, as the mare fled up and over a hill. Slowly Hump gained on the wild horse. Closer he came, and closer. Suddenly he thrust out his

pole with
its noose on the end.
The noose settled on the
wild mare's neck and he pulled
it tight.

With a shrill whinny and a snort of defiance, the mare reared up. Hump pulled the noose still tighter. A moment later, gasping for breath, she staggered and fell. Instantly, Hump and Curly were both on the ground beside her.

"Watch out for her feet," Hump warned quietly, as he fastened his rope securely around the mare's nose. "Back my horse over here, Curly."

Curly obeyed and Hump quickly tied the other end of his rope to his own horse, fasten-

[44]

ing it to the tail and around the shoulders. Then he loosened the noose, which was choking the little wild mare. The mare jumped up and tried to jerk away. But the rope was strong and Hump's horse had been well trained.

Before long, Hump and Curly were able to start home, with Hump on his big black horse, pulling the weary little mare along. Other men were also riding back to the village with the animals they had captured. Curly looked the wild horses over as he trotted along beside Hump. Some of them were bigger and stronger than the sorrel mare, but none was more beautiful or spirited.

"She'd make a fast buffalo horse," Curly remarked when they were almost home. "Is that what you're planning to use her for?"

"I'm not planning to use her at all," Hump said. "If you can train her, younger brother, she's yours."

"Mine!" Curly's heart leaped for joy. He tried to thank Hump, but the words would not come. "I'll—I'll call her Red Streak," he said. "And I'll try to train her so she'll be as good a horse as your big black stallion."

Hump smiled and said nothing. When they reached the village he called Lean Elk to help him throw the wild mare. Then they hobbled her feet and let her get up.

For the next few days, Curly was very busy trying to tame and break his wild mare. At last the time came when Hump said he could ride her. Talking to her quietly, Curly took hold of her mane. Suddenly he swung himself to her back.

"Stick fast!" Hump shouted as the horse bucked. And Curly stuck, though his heart was in his mouth.

Plunging and snorting, the horse tried to shake him off, but the boy clung to her neck, lying low. Finally she stopped bucking and stood still. Then Curly kicked her sides with his moccasined heels.

"*Hoka hey!*" he shouted, as she broke into a gallop and headed for the sand hills. "*Hoka hey!*"

She ran like the wind. Flecks of foam flew from her mouth. On and on she sped until she was too tired to keep up the mad gallop any longer. When she stopped at last, she was trembling all over. Curly, too, was trembling. His body was bruised and shaken, but he had never been happier.

Without giving Red Streak a chance to rest,

he pushed his knee hard against her side, until she turned to get away from the pressure and headed for the village.

Every day after that, for several moons, Curly worked with Red Streak. He taught her to come when he whistled and to obey his commands. He practiced springing to the ground when she was galloping and then springing up again into the saddle. He learned to slide from one side of her body to the other, as warriors did in battle, riding so low that only his heel showed over her back.

Every day, also, he practiced with his bow and arrows. And one evening, in the Moon of Grass Appearing, when the Oglalas were camping near Bear Butte, Hump called him into his tepee.

"You have a good horse, and your arms are now as strong as your bow," Hump said. "Tomorrow the scouts will set out in search of buffalo. When they find a large herd—" He smiled.

"I can go on the hunt?" Curly asked eagerly.

Hump nodded. And Curly sped home joyfully to tell his family the good news.

CHAPTER FIVE

The Buffalo Hunt

Bright STAR filled the big horn spoon with deer-meat stew and held it out to Curly. But her brother shook his head.

"Eat," urged his mother, who stood near the cooking fire outside the tepee. "Buffalo hunters need strength."

Curly grinned and took the spoon. He tried to eat, although he was not hungry.

Little Hawk watched him curiously. "Are you afraid?" he asked.

"All boys are afraid when they first hunt buffalo," Curly admitted, swallowing a mouthful of meat. "But they forget about it soon after the hunt begins. That's what Hump told me."

He took another piece of meat from the spoon and popped it into his mouth. "I'm go-

ing to get Red Streak," he said, handing the
spoon back to his sister.

As he set off at a run toward the valley
where the horses were grazing, his mother
looked after him fondly. He seemed too young
and too small to hunt buffalo. Suppose he
should be trampled or gored when he rode
among the great shaggy creatures?

"It's better not to think of it," she told herself. And she went into the tepee to get Curly's
bow and arrows. When he came galloping
back on Red Streak, she handed them up to
him.

Just then Curly's father came down from
the ridge where he had been praying and
smoking his sacred pipe.

"Take care today, my son," he said, laying
his hand on the boy's knee. "Remember that
on a first hunt it is wise to try only for calves."

"I'll remember," Curly promised quickly.
"But I want to bring home plenty of meat
and—"

"And some hides, too," Little Hawk called
from the entrance to the tepee. "Then we can
trade one for white-man knives when we go
to the fort this summer. Look, Curly. The
akicita are lining up. Better make haste."

[49]

Curly glanced over his shoulder. It was true! The *akicita,* who kept order in the village, had already drawn up their horses in a long row. And the hunters were riding up behind them five abreast, each leading his buffalo horse.

Curly pounded his heels against Red Streak's ribs. Calling good-by to his family, he rode off swiftly to join the long column. Lone Bear and He Dog, who were also going on their first hunt, came galloping up to meet him.

"Hump's leading us!" He Dog cried excitedly.

Curly nodded. He could see Hump sitting on his horse at the head of the line, waiting to give the signal to start.

Finally everyone was ready. First in line were the *akicita,* with the sun shining on their long lances and feathered head-dresses. Next were the hunters with their well-trained buffalo horses. And last the younger boys like Curly, impatient to be on their way.

Hump swung his horse around, gave a signal, and the big hunting party began to move forward. Old men, women, and many children came running up to shout good-by.

Curly's eyes shone as he waved his arm at Bright Star and Little Hawk and his mother, who were all calling his name. Then he turned and sat tall on his horse, trying to act as though he were not in the least excited.

The buffalo herd which the scouts had found was a half a day's journey from the village. The sun was warm and the men rode slowly over rolling hills and across open country. Now and then an impatient young warrior left his place in line and tried to gallop ahead. But the *akicita* always stopped him and sent him back, so that he would not frighten the buffalo and spoil the hunt. And when Fat Beaver tried this trick a second time, one of the *akicita* caught him, broke his bow, and ordered him to go home.

"It serves him right," Lone Bear muttered as Fat Beaver passed them on his way back to the village, looking very glum.

But Curly hardly heard him. His eyes were on Hump, who was riding ahead up a steep hill. On the crest of the hill, the warrior halted and raised his hand.

"Hump has seen the buffalo!" Curly exclaimed softly. And his heart began to pound as the column came to a stop.

The hunters dismounted quietly and slipped walking hobbles on the horses they had been riding. Then they mounted their barebacked buffalo horses. Obeying signals which Hump gave them, they rode off slowly in two long lines to surround the herd.

He Dog and Lone Bear were riding with their fathers now, and Curly rode Red Streak beside Hump's beautiful black buffalo horse. As he reached the brow of the hill, he drew his breath in sharply. His hand tightened on his bow.

Never before had he seen so many buffalo. The plain below was dark with them. With lowered heads, huge shaggy bulls, fat cows, and red-brown calves were cropping the short spring grass. None of them seemed to sense

[52]

that danger was near as the hunters silently surrounded them.

"It should be a good hunt," Hump remarked quietly to Curly. "Ride close to the buffalo and pull hard on your bow. Don't forget that if blood comes from an animal's mouth it will die, and you can go on to kill another."

Curly stared down at the great herd of buffalo and said nothing. He was too excited to speak. Suddenly Hump gave the hunters another signal.

"*Hoka hey!*" he shouted, starting downhill at a gallop, with his bow held high.

"*Hoka hey!*" Curly screamed shrilly, racing behind him on Red Streak.

"Yi-yi-yi!" yelled the hunters, closing in on the buffalo from all sides. "*Hoka hey!*"

Arrows whizzed through the air. Some buffalo fell with blood streaming from their mouths. Others, terrified, began to run.

"*Yihoo!*" shouted the hunters whenever a buffalo staggered and fell. "*Yihoo! Yihoo! Yihoo!*"

Curly's heart was thudding like a war drum. He leaned forward on his galloping mare, gripping his bow and trying to see through

[53]

the great clouds of dust. His ears rang with the thunder of hoofs, the rattle of horns as the buffalo collided with one another, and the cries of the hunters.

A huge cow rushed by him, almost knocking him from his horse. Red Streak darted swiftly to one side. Curly lay low on her back. For a moment he was terrified.

If only he could get clear of the blinding dust! There! Now it was behind him! An angry bull tore past, brushing against his leg. A calf ran behind the bull, bellowing with fear.

Curly yanked an arrow from his quiver. He aimed for the calf and missed, but hit the bull in the hump. Shaking his horns, the bull galloped on, while the calf darted off in another direction. For an instant Curly hesitated. He

remembered his father's words: "It is wise to try only for calves."

"But I can kill a bull," the boy thought, with a sudden feeling of power. And he raced after the wounded buffalo. Clinging to Red Streak with his knees, he shot again and hit the bull in the flank. Still the great beast ran on.

"Faster, Red Streak!" Curly shouted. "Faster!"

The brave little mare responded. In a burst of speed she overtook the big buffalo, coming up close on his right side. Once more Curly's bowstring twanged. His arrow sank deep into the shaggy body, almost up to the feathers on the shaft.

"*Yihoo!*" yelled Curly triumphantly, as Red Streak carried him past the buffalo. "*Yihoo!*"

Sure that he had made a kill, he turned, expecting to see the buffalo fall. But, with lowered head, the bull was charging straight at Red Streak.

The little mare swerved to get out of the way. Suddenly she stumbled and Curly tightened the grip of his knees. He knew that if she fell they might both be trampled or gored.

But the mare kept her footing. With the speed of lightning, Curly sent another arrow deep into the bull's body. The buffalo slowed down and finally stood still, bewildered. Blood began to stream from its mouth and nose. A moment later the powerful animal took a few staggering steps. Then its legs buckled under it. With a great sigh, it sank slowly to the ground.

Curly slid from the back of his horse. Her sides were heaving and she was white with foam.

"We did it!" Curly said joyfully, patting her neck.

All about him on the wide plain, hunters were shouting triumphantly over dead or dying buffalo. Some of the men had already begun the work of butchering. Curly had never cut up a buffalo, but he decided to try it. Pulling his knife from his belt, he went up to the bull, uncertain where to begin. At that moment Hump's hand was laid on his shoulder.

"Is this your bull?" the warrior asked.

"Yes," Curly said proudly. Then he looked a little crestfallen. "But I had to use four arrows, Hump, and I wish I had killed it with one."

[57]

Hump smiled. "A boy on his first hunt who kills a buffalo with one arrow, Curly, is just lucky," he said. "But a boy who chases an angry bull and drives four arrows into him has a brave heart. I am well pleased with you, younger brother."

When Curly reached home, later that day, he found that his father, also, was pleased with him. And his mother was overjoyed.

"Now we have a real hunter in our family," she cried proudly as she unloaded the meat from Red Streak's back. "I know that the people in our tepee will never lack for food."

For the rest of that day the women were busy cutting buffalo meat into thin strips and hanging them on the drying racks outside the tepees. And that night the people of the village prepared for a fine feast. Cooking fires blazed and the air was filled with the good smells of roasting humps and ribs.

When Curly had eaten until he couldn't hold another mouthful, he danced in the circle with everyone else, to the steady beating of drums. Then came the time for which most of the boys had been waiting. The time when fathers would sing of the brave deeds of their sons.

He Dog's father walked from tepee to tepee singing about his boy, who had killed a fat calf on his first buffalo hunt. And He Dog stood up proudly in the firelight while the people called his name. Lone Bear, too, stood up after his father's song of praise, for he also had shot a calf. Then Hump started around the wide circle singing in his deep voice of Curly, who, with a brave heart, had chased and killed a fine big bull.

"Curly!" the people shouted. "Curly!" And they waited for Curly to step forward into the firelight.

But Curly sat still in the shadow of his father's tepee, telling himself that it was no great thing for a boy to kill a buffalo.

"I wish I could get a chance to do something braver than that," he thought.

Before many moons had passed, his wish came true.

CHAPTER SIX

All Because of a Cow

THE sun beat down on the white-man road. The flag over Fort Laramie hung limp. In the big Indian encampment, three miles east of the fort, old people drowsed in the shade of the tepees. Women talked softly as they went about their work. And the children played quietly, because of the heat.

Three big circles of tepees had been set up between the road and the broad, shallow Platte River. The Oglalas' village was nearest the fort. Then came the Minniconjou village. And beyond that were the Brulés.

In the Brulé village, Curly was watching his uncle, Spotted Tail, paint a war shield. At last, the man glanced up from his work.

"Go and look again," he said to Curly.

Curly walked out to the dusty road. Shading his eyes, he peered to the east. Then he strolled back to the tepee.

"There's a wagon train coming," he told his uncle. "But it's just some more of those whites called Mormons. I can't see anything else."

Spotted Tail grunted. "Two moons we've been here," he grumbled, getting to his feet. "And all the while the presents which the whites owe us have been stored in the trading house. Does the Great White Father think we have nothing to do but loaf in the sun, waiting for the agent to come to distribute them? It's time we went back to the buffalo country."

"Red Cloud's gone back," Curly remarked, slapping at a mosquito which was buzzing near his ear. "He said no white-man presents were worth waiting for so long. But Smoke wants the coffee that's coming to him, and the sugar and—"

"And so do many others," Spotted Tail added. He ducked through the entrance of the tepee, carrying his shield with care. Curly wandered back to the road, wishing that something exciting would happen.

The Mormons' wagon train passed him slowly in a cloud of dust. There were only a few wagons and they were small and shabby. Some distance behind them, a man hurried along, driving a scrawny old cow. Curly watched him hit the animal again and again with a long stick.

"The poor cow's so tired she can't move any faster," Curly thought. But he was wrong.

At that moment, five Brulé boys came tearing across the plain on their ponies, yelling and whooping as they tried to see who could reach the road first.

Frightened by this sudden noise, the cow threw up her tail and bolted right into the Brulé village. Running across the wide circle, she plunged into one of the tepees and came out through the other side with a bundle caught on her horns. Curly and some of the other boys chased her, howling with glee.

Kicking up her heels, she galloped past another tepee, upsetting a shield stand, trampling a drum, and knocking over a kettle of stew. By this time the whole village had come to life. Dogs barked excitedly. Women screamed at their children to get out of the way. And the men roared with laughter.

One of those who laughed was a young Minniconjou named Straight Foretop. He had

Curly and the other boys chased her, howling with glee

come to show some of his Brulé friends the long rifle which had cost him many hides at the trading house. Now he pointed his gun at the cow, intending to kill her before she did any more damage. But Spotted Tail shouted a warning.

"Be careful! That's a white man's cow!"

"It isn't now," cried Black Beaver. "The Mormon ran off and left it here."

"There goes another shield stand!" called a wrinkled old squaw. "Shoot the cow before she hurts anybody. Shoot her!"

Straight Foretop took careful aim and fired. The old cow dropped to the ground, dead. Soon two of the Brulés began to butcher it and to divide the meat among some of the women. Then Curly ran to get his horse, which was tied near his uncle's tepee, and rode home to tell his family about the funny thing that had happened in the Brulé village.

The story of the runaway cow was told in many tepees that day. People chuckled over it and then forgot all about it. But early in the evening, the trader, old Jim Bordeaux, who had married a Brulé, rode into the Oglala village. He was not as jolly as he usually was when he visited his Indian friends.

"That Mormon has been making bad talk about the cow that Straight Foretop shot," he told the Oglalas who gathered around him. "He stopped in at my place this afternoon to get some water, and he swore the cow had been stolen from him."

"But it wasn't," Curly protested. "I saw the whole thing and—"

"I know all about what happened," Bordeaux said, mopping his bearded face with a red handkerchief. "But that Mormon's a mean man, and he wants to stir up trouble. When he gets to the fort he's going to tell the lieutenant that you people stole the cow and ought to be punished. That new lieutenant's not friendly to Indians the way Colonel Mitchell was. Maybe one of the chiefs should ride to the fort tomorrow to talk with him."

"Conquering Bear of the Brulés is the man to do that," said old Chief Smoke. "At the Treaty Council, Mitchell made him our Paper Chief to speak for all of us. I'll send a message to him now. And there will be no trouble with the whites, my friend. This matter of a weak old cow is nothing."

That evening a message was sent to Conquering Bear. And the next day when Curly was teaching Little Hawk some wrestling holds near the road, the Paper Chief passed them on his way to the fort. In spite of the heat, he was proudly wearing the gold-trimmed officer's coat which had been given to him at the Treaty Council. And he rode his finest horse.

It was nearly sunset when he came back and turned into the Oglala village to tell everyone what had happened at the fort. As the people gathered about him, thunderclouds were piling up in the west and the sky was streaked with lightning.

"My news is like this storm that threatens," Conquering Bear told the Oglalas. "Today I talked long with the white soldier-chief. But it was that bad half-breed, Wyuse, who put my words into the white man's tongue. He may have said things I did not say. For the white chief became red-angry. He shouted at me that I must take Straight Foretop to him to be locked up in the iron jail."

"Because of an old skinny cow!" cried Curly, forgetting in his eagerness that a boy should never interrupt a chief.

Conquering Bear nodded slowly and his fur-wrapped braids swung back and forth.

"Because of a cow," he said, raising his voice as thunder rumbled in the distance. "And there is worse news. I offered to give the best horse in my herd to pay for that cow. I said I could not bring Straight Foretop to the fort because he was a guest in our village when he shot the cow. I tried to explain that our people never make a guest do anything against his will. But the white chief would not listen. Tomorrow he will send soldiers to our camp to arrest the Minniconjou."

"Soldiers!"

There was a moment of shocked silence.

Then everybody began to talk at once, as Conquering Bear turned his horse and rode away toward the Brulé village.

A gust of wind sent dust swirling through the camp. Chief Smoke pulled his blanket around his shoulders and began to speak to his people.

"The whites made big talk about peace at the Treaty Council," he said. "I do not think they will send soldiers into a village where there are helpless women and children. Nor would they take away a man's freedom because of a cow."

"If they do, it will be the fault of that half-breed, Wyuse," called someone in the crowd. "He drinks too much white-man firewater and twists our words when he puts them into the white-man tongue."

"*Hou,*" agreed Hump, who stood near Smoke with his hand on Curly's shoulder. "Someone else should go to the fort. Man Afraid knows a little of the white-man language. Perhaps he can make the white chief listen."

Smoke turned to a tall, fine-looking warrior.

"Will you go to the fort tomorrow, my friend?" he asked. "Can you make strong talk to the white chief about this bad thing he is planning?"

"Yes," Man Afraid said. "I will go—"

A crash of thunder drowned the rest of his words. Lightning flashed across the darkening sky and the storm broke in a great rush of rain.

People began running for shelter. Curly raced home to help his mother lower the tepee walls which had been raised because of the heat. With a big stone hammer, he pounded down the stakes which held the tepee covering to the ground.

As he worked, the cooling rain pelted down on him and the wind tossed his hair. When he had pounded in the last stake, he straightened up and faced the full fury of the storm. He had always liked such storms. They filled him with excitement and a sense of strength, as though he were part of the earth and the sky. For a moment he stood still, wondering why this was so. Then suddenly he remembered Straight Foretop.

"A man in an iron jail could never feel the wind or the rain," he thought with a shiver.

And, ducking under the flap over the entrance of the tepee, he went inside to put away his hammer.

[69]

CHAPTER SEVEN

"Don't Shoot My People!"

CURLY tossed and turned on his bed that night, thinking about Straight Foretop and wondering if the soldiers would really come. It was late when he fell asleep, but he woke before sunrise. Creeping from the tepee, he walked down to the river. He was restless and unhappy, and he didn't know why.

"I wish I were tall and strong like Hump," he thought impatiently. "Growing up takes so long! I want to be a warrior *now!*"

Picking up a stone, he hurled it into the river.

"If those whites take Straight Foretop to-day," he said aloud, "I'll— I'll—"

"Who do you think you're talking to?" asked someone behind him.

Curly swung around. He grinned sheepishly when he saw Lone Bear laughing at him from a clump of young willow trees.

"Come on, old Chief Talks-to-Himself," said Lone Bear. "Man Afraid's going to the fort soon. Let's hide in that gully where we killed the rattlesnakes. Then we'll be the first to see him come back. And we'll find out what happened before anyone else does."

"All right," agreed Curly. "Let's go."

The boys ran back to their village. They hastily ate some morning meat, got their bows and arrows, and unhobbled their horses.

Soon they were crouching in the gravel of a dry gully. As the hot sun crawled slowly up the sky, yellow jackets buzzed angrily about their heads. A large green lizard slid from behind a rock near Curly's feet and darted away. Horseflies settled on the ponies, making them stamp and flick their tails. But the boys barely moved as they watched the road, waiting to see Man Afraid come riding back over the ridge. At last Lone Bear spoke.

"He's been gone a long time," he said uneasily. "I wonder what the soldiers will do to Straight Foretop if they arrest him. Will they chain his arms and legs?"

Curly shook his head. "I don't know," he

replied. "But no white man will ever lock *me* up! Never! I'd kill the man who tried it!"

He brushed his hair back from his eyes. "Why do they think they're so big?" he went on impatiently. "This is *our* country! What do they—" He drew his breath in sharply.

"Look!" he cried. "Man Afraid has failed —and here they come."

A wagon filled with soldiers had stopped on the ridge. For a moment it stood there, sharp against the sky. Then an officer on horseback waved his gleaming sword. The wagon started down the road and the boys saw that it was followed by two small cannon on wheels, pulled by horses. Behind the cannon, Man Afraid rode alone, his head hanging as if he were in despair.

[72]

Curly and Lone Bear mounted quickly and headed for their village.

"Blue Coats!" they shouted, galloping into the Oglala circle. "Blue Coats! They're coming with wagon guns!"

To their surprise they found that scouts had already signaled this and other news to the Oglalas. Hump called the two boys to him.

"The Blue Coat with the sword is Grattan," Hump said quietly. "He's the loud-talking man who doesn't like Indians. Wyuse is with him and he's drunk again on firewater. We must have all the horses near us in case of trouble. Go and tell the herd boys to bring them to the bottom land between the camps and the river."

Almost before Hump had finished speaking, Curly and Lone Bear were on their way. Splashing across the shallow river, they galloped for the hills where the big herds were grazing. Whooping and waving their arms, they helped drive the horses down the hills and across the river to the bottom land behind the encampment. Then they rode on toward the Brulé village, determined to see what the soldiers would do.

At the bottom of the shelving bank, just behind the village, they stopped and tied their horses to some bushes. Women and children were already hurrying from the village to wait in the willows near the river until the soldiers had come and gone. Men followed them, not painted for war, but carrying spears and bows and arrows. The warriors crawled into the bushes just under the edge of the bank, where they could see everything that went on in the village.

"The warriors are all ready for trouble," said Curly. "Let's climb up there with them. If there's a fight, I want to get into it."

"So do I," Lone Bear replied. "Look out! There's your uncle, Spotted Tail. If he sees us, he'll send us down to the willows."

Curly dropped to the ground at once. So did Lone Bear. The boys worked their way silently up the bank and into a tangle of chokeberry bushes near the top. As they peered over the edge, they saw Grattan lead his blue-coated soldiers into the Brulé camp.

The soldiers were on foot now. Several of them were pulling the two cannon. Wyuse was still on horseback. Slapping his hand against his mouth, he rode around the circle, making war whoops and shouting.

"Come on out, you filthy redskins," he cried in a voice hoarse with too much whisky. "Come out of your holes! We'll kill you like dogs and eat your hearts raw! Come on, you red devils, come out!"

Grattan shouted an order to his soldiers, who put the cannon in place and took up their positions. Then he looked around the camp.

Straight Foretop, the Minniconjou, was standing in the entrance of one of the tepees, leaning on his gun. Near him, chiefs and head-men from each village stood quietly, with their blankets wrapped proudly around them. Conquering Bear was in the group, his hands empty of weapons. Slowly he walked toward Grattan.

"Take your soldiers back to the fort, my friend," he said, "and leave us in peace. We will give you five horses—the best in our herds—to pay for that skinny cow. But don't try to arrest the Minniconjou."

"They can't arrest me," Straight Foretop called from the tepee. "They will never lock me up in their prison, for I will die first. But take your people away, Conquering Bear, so that none will be hurt if there is fighting."

At these words, Curly gripped Lone Bear's

arm. "He's brave," he whispered. "Now Wyuse is putting his words into the white-man tongue."

Leaning from his saddle, the drunken Wyuse was shouting at Grattan. Suddenly the young lieutenant's face flamed. He snapped

out an order. The soldiers raised their guns. One of them fired and hit Conquering Bear's brother, who was standing with the head-men. Conquering Bear ran forward.

"Don't shoot my people!" he cried. "And you Brulés back there! Hold your arrows! Don't fight! We can still settle this peacefully. White men, don't shoot again!"

But Grattan was already shouting another order and helping to aim the cannon. Sud-

denly there were two loud booms and the rattle of musket fire. With blood streaming from three wounds, brave Conquering Bear fell forward, just as cannon balls tore into the tepees.

An instant later, Straight Foretop raised his rifle and fired through the smoke. Grattan staggered, clutching his side, and a wave of angry warriors swarmed over the bank. Some of the Blue Coats were killed on the spot. Others fled down the road, with howling warriors hot on their heels.

Curly had wanted to rush out and join the fighting. But he felt weak and queer. Lone Bear seemed to feel that way, too. The boys had never seen men killed before.

"Are you afraid?" Lone Bear asked shakily, as he peered through the bushes at the bodies lying on the ground.

"No," answered Curly. "I don't know how I feel. I wanted to do something brave. But I didn't."

"You can now," said Lone Bear. "And I can, too. I dare you to count coup on the dead men."

Without a word Curly scrambled to his feet and darted over the top of the bank into the Brulé village. Lone Bear followed close behind him. They paid no attention to the yelling warriors, but ran here and there, touching each of the bloody bodies sprawled on the earth.

"I, the brave Curly, have counted coup on the cowardly whites!" cried Curly at last.

"I, too, have counted coup on every one of them," screamed Lone Bear. "And I have kicked the dead Wyuse!"

By this time, warriors from the other villages were streaming into the Brulé camp. Hump caught Curly by the shoulder.

"Quick, younger brother," he said, "and you, too, Lone Bear. Get back to your own village. Help the women take down the tepees. Help them pack the travois. We're going to—"

"Is Conquering Bear dead?" Curly interrupted anxiously.

"Not one of our people is dead," Hump hastily replied. "But Grattan's men have all been killed. No one knows what will happen now. And we're heading for the hills."

CHAPTER EIGHT

Curly Is Puzzled

PEOPLE spoke softly in the village which the Indians had set up on the banks of Running Water. In the tepee of Conquering Bear, the medicine man was praying.

The three boys who crouched behind the tepee could hear him chanting and shaking his rattle. When he stopped, Little Hawk whispered to his brother.

"Will the chief die soon, Curly?" he asked.

Curly nodded solemnly. "Father says his life will melt like snow in summer," he replied softly. "It will not last many days and—"

"Shh!" said Little Big Man. "Conquering Bear is speaking."

The boys moved closer to listen. At first the voice of the wounded chief was so feeble that they could not make out his words. Then it grew stronger.

[*80*]

"Remember," they heard him say. "Do not —be angry with the whites when I am gone. Do not let—our young men fight them. It will bring more trouble—more—"

He moaned pitifully, and Curly's heart grew tight at the thought of his suffering. Without a word to the other boys, he stood up and walked swiftly to the tree where Red Streak was tied. Mounting the horse, he started to ride away from the village.

Little Big Man ran after him. "Curly," he cried, "where are you going?"

"Nowhere," Curly called back, "and I don't want anyone with me."

Turning Red Streak toward the west, he rode until he had reached the top of a hill some distance from the river. There he dismounted, put walking hobbles on the mare, and threw himself on the ground. He had no idea why he had left the village so suddenly. He knew only that he wanted to be alone.

So many puzzling things had happened. He needed time to think about them. And this was a good place to do it—here, under the wide blue sky with no company but his horse and a little red-backed hawk swaying on a thistle.

In his mind Curly began to go over the events of the past few days. First, there had been the foolish cow trouble. After that, the terrible fighting in the Brulé village. Next, the flight to the hills, with six strong men carrying the wounded Paper Chief in a buffalo-hide sling.

Then a horde of angry warriors had ridden back to the trading houses. They had broken down the doors and taken all the presents for which the Indians had been waiting so long. Meanwhile, scouts had kept a sharp lookout along the white-man road for more soldiers with wagon guns. But none had come.

"Maybe the whites are afraid of us now," Curly thought. "Maybe they'll get out of our country and leave us alone. I wish I knew."

Suddenly he longed to be wise, like his father. There were so many things he needed to know, particularly about himself. He had counted coup on the whites, but only because Lone Bear had dared him to do it. Would he ever be really brave? He knew that sometimes men found answers to such questions in dreams.

"I shall stay here fasting and praying until a vision comes to me," he decided.

He stood up and the little red-backed hawk flew off toward the river. Red Streak had made her way down the hill in search of grass. Now he was quite alone. Lifting his face, Curly prayed.

"Send me a vision, great *Wakan Tanka*," he begged. "Send me a vision."

For a long time he stood there, almost expecting to see a dark kindly face look down from the sky. But nothing happened. The sun sank, the wind grew chill, and the stars appeared. Feeling very small, alone on the hill, Curly watched a half-eaten moon begin its slow walk down the sky.

At last he lay down, with sharp little stones piled under his back to keep him from falling asleep. As the night dragged on, he tried to lift his thoughts to the world beyond this one, praying again for a vision.

Morning came, bringing a hot sun, hunger, and thirst, but no vision. By midday the boy had begun to feel weak and ill. He thought that the blazing afternoon would never end. Slowly the cruel sun walked down the western sky and vanished at last behind the hills, leaving an afterglow of pink and gold.

Suddenly, all the world was blackness. Then

[*83*]

the sky seemed to split in two and there was a great blinding light. The vision had come!

Out of the sky a mighty warrior was riding toward the earth on a giant bay horse. He wore sky-blue leggings. A red-backed hawk was caught in his streaming hair. One bright zigzag lightning flash was painted on his right cheek and there were blue hailstones painted on his chest. A brown pebble was tied behind one of his ears.

People crowded close behind him. And as his bay horse galloped down from the heavens, its color changed to black, then to white, then red spots magically covered its body. Nearer it came and nearer. And Curly saw a great host of ghostlike enemies rush out, firing guns and sending clouds of arrows whizzing toward the warrior rider. But the warrior rode forward through his enemies, unharmed.

Then one man leaped up quickly from behind and seized the warrior's body! And in that instant Curly *was* the warrior, struggling to free himself. There was a loud shouting in his ears and he opened his eyes. His father was standing over him, shaking him by the shoulder.

"What foolishness is this?" the holy man demanded angrily. "Running away at such a time! Hump and I have searched two days for you when we should have been at the side of our dying Paper Chief. Why did you do this thoughtless thing?"

Curly sat up, rubbing his eyes, too bewildered to speak. "I didn't run away," he finally protested. Weakly he added, "I had a reason for staying here on the hill. I—"

The tall shadowy figure of Hump suddenly appeared over the rim of the hill. The warrior was leading Red Streak.

"Get up, younger brother," he said gruffly. "Get on your horse. It is nearly night."

Without a word, the boy obeyed, though he was so weary he could hardly climb to his horse's back. The three rode home in silence. Curly wanted to tell about his vision and to ask what it meant. But he knew that now was not the time, and he was almost too tired to care.

When they reached the village, he had little to say to his mother. And later he pushed aside the soup which she tried to give him. His father looked at him questioningly.

"What is wrong with you, Curly?" he asked.

Again Curly wanted to speak of his vision,

[*85*]

but the words would not come. A lump rose in his throat.

"Father," he cried unhappily, "why did you and Hump scold me as if I were still a little papoose? Why am I still called Curly—a silly baby name? I'm nearly thirteen snows old now! I'm— I'm a man!"

His father smiled. "A boy is a boy until he proves he is a man," he said in a kindly voice. "Then he is given his man-name. You know that, my son. Now go to your sleeping robes."

Stumbling across the tepee, Curly obeyed and fell asleep at once.

At dawn he was awakened by the sound of women wailing. Brave Conquering Bear, the Paper Chief, was dead. Later that day, Curly helped Hump and three other men to build a high platform on a green hill overlooking Running Water. And on the platform the body of the good chief was laid to rest, dressed in his finest robes, with his war bonnet and his shield at his side.

Now that the chief was gone, there was no reason for the Indians to camp anywhere near the white-man road, where trouble had walked and might walk again. The Minniconjous and the Oglalas headed north, and the Brulés set out for White Earth River, to the northeast. Curly's family went with the Brulés so that his mother could be with her own people for a while.

Little Thunder, the Brulé chief, chose a fine spot for the winter camp. There were many buffalo and hunting was good. The men brought their horses home loaded with hides and meat. The women made new tepee coverings, fur-lined moccasins, and shirts. The children gathered wild plums and berries to be dried and stored in parfleches. And everyone was so busy getting ready for the cold days ahead that the cow trouble was almost forgotten.

But one day in the Moon of Falling Leaves, Curly and his brother saw their uncle, Spotted Tail, streaking his face with war paint. They were not surprised, for now that the whites had broken their treaty promise, the Indians were not bound to keep peace with their enemies. But the boys were curious.

"Are you going against the Crows?" asked Little Hawk.

"Against the whites," replied Spotted Tail, as he quickly fastened a feather in his hair.

"The whites!" exclaimed Little Hawk.

"But Conquering Bear told us never to fight the whites! We heard him, didn't we, Curly?"

Curly nodded as Spotted Tail arose and picked up his war shield.

"A chief's death must always be avenged," said Spotted Tail, reaching for his bow. "That is the custom of our people."

He strode toward four other warriors who stood waiting for him near Little Thunder's tepee. In a short time they were riding proudly away from the village, singing brave-heart war songs. Curly watched them disappear over the hills, longing to be with them.

None of the Indians in that part of the country had ever before sent out a war party against the whites. And there were many Brulés who were troubled to see the warriors go. But others said, "It was the whites who started the fighting. They threw away their treaty promise and killed the chief whom they themselves had chosen. We cannot be their friends again until someone has paid for the suffering of good Conquering Bear."

Day after day, the people in the village waited anxiously for the return of the little war party. At last one evening the warriors came riding back. Snow was falling and the north wind was cold, so everyone crowded into the council lodge to hear what had happened. Spotted Tail began the story.

"We hid near the white-man road not far from the place of the cow trouble, until a wagon came along," he said. "It was the kind the whites call 'mail-coach.' We killed the driver and the man beside him, but let the man inside the wagon get away. Then we opened an iron box. It was filled with round

pieces of gold and silver, and many, many pieces of green paper."

He stopped to light his pipe and a man named Long Chin took up the story.

"The green paper was good for nothing," Long Chin went on, "so we let the wind take it. But we kept the gold and silver."

"And what is that good for except to wear in your hair?" cried an old man, sitting far back in the shadows.

"For trading with the whites," said Spotted Tail. "Some traders will give us guns for it. Jim Bordeaux told us so when we stopped to see him on our way home."

"Weren't there any soldiers around?" asked Crazy Horse. "Didn't you see any Blue Coats anywhere?"

"Bordeaux said there were many new soldiers at the fort," answered Spotted Tail. "We saw some of them a long way off. But none came after us as we rode home."

"That is good," said Little Thunder quietly. "The death of our Paper Chief has been avenged. The trouble of the cow is over."

And for nine happy moons Little Thunder and his people believed that this was so. Then a terrible thing happened to the Brulés.

CHAPTER NINE

A Dreadful Day

ALL Indians who are friendly to the whites must move south of the Platte River at once!"

Little Thunder looked gravely at Goose, the man who had brought this message from Fort Laramie.

"I do not understand, Goose," said the chief slowly. "Who has said this?"

"The new soldier-chief at the fort," replied Goose. "A man with white hair on his face, named Harney. He wants to know whether you are going to move or not. I must go back to the fort and give him your answer. There are many soldiers at the fort now—many."

Little Thunder nodded slowly. Then he looked at the drying racks, heavy with freshly killed buffalo meat, and at the women busily scraping skins. The new camp on Blue Water

Creek was north of the Platte, but a long way from Fort Laramie. Why should the white soldier-chief want the Brulés to move? Had not the Brulés always been friendly to the whites, except for the old cow trouble? Little Thunder turned to Goose.

"Tell the White-Beard Chief that I do not think I should move my people in hot weather while meat and skins are drying," he said. "It would be foolish to do this just to prove that we are at peace."

He called to one of the women and asked her to bring Goose some food. Then he gave the man a fresh horse, and Goose rode back to the fort.

A few days after his visit, Curly and his Brulé friend, High Shirt, decided to look for wild horses among the sand hills to the northeast. They galloped out of the village just as the sun rose. Late that afternoon, tired and hot, they started home.

As they rounded the top of a high hill several miles from the village, they pulled up their horses suddenly. They stared in dismay toward the place where the village lay hidden behind a ridge. A great cloud of black smoke was rolling upward, high into the sky.

"That smoke's not coming from cooking-fires!" cried Curly. "There's too much of it. Our village must be burning up! Maybe the Crows have attacked it, or—"

"Or the whites!" interrupted High Shirt, with a note of fear in his voice. "Curly, I—I'm not going back with you."

Curly stared at High Shirt. "If you're afraid of the whites, you're a coward and you are my friend no longer," he said hotly. And before the older boy could speak, Curly was halfway down the hill. His fast little mare seemed to know that something was wrong, and she covered the ground with the speed of the north wind in winter.

She was panting and covered with lather when Curly stopped her at the foot of the ridge behind the Brulé camp. He tied her to a scrub oak and looked about warily. No sounds came from the village. Dropping to his knees, he laid his ear to the ground. Far to the south he could hear the thud-thud made by the feet of marching men.

"Whites!" he thought angrily. "They're headed for the road to the fort."

He wriggled his way up the ridge, moving as silently as a snake, fearing that some whites might still be lurking near by. Peering over the top of the ridge, he stared down as though he could not believe his eyes.

That morning he had left a village filled with busy, happy people. Now there *was* no village! Only smoldering piles of ashes, smoking bundles of half-burned hides, a few charred parfleches, and some blackened meat on the ground.

Leaping to his feet, he ran swiftly down the ridge and through the ruined camp, looking for some sign of life. There was none. Quickly he stooped to study the ground in the twilight. It was covered with tracks made by wheels, horses' hoofs, soldiers' boots, moccasins, and travois, all mixed up together. Some of the tracks led south and some led to the northeast. Which trail should he follow?

"The moccasin tracks going south mean some of the Brulés have been captured," he thought. "The others have all fled, with the soldiers hot on their heels. They'll make a stand somewhere, and I will help them fight."

Scrambling over the ridge, he mounted Red Streak and set out to the northeast. For some time he followed the trail through the deepening shadows. Then suddenly, at the foot of a sandstone bluff, Red Streak balked and snorted with fear. Curly choked back a cry of horror at the sight before him.

The bluff was strewn with lifeless Indian bodies, and there were signs of what must have been a terrible fight. Sliding from Red Streak's back, Curly ran quickly from one body to another, stooping to peer into each face—dreading what he might find. Here were children who had been playing happily on the banks of Blue Water that very morning—and old men —and many women. Most of them had been scalped by the white soldiers. Curly was sickened by the terrible sight, even though he found no one from his own family and no close friend.

He saw that the soldiers' trail now turned to the west. The Blue Coats had not followed the Indians beyond this point. But where were the Brulés who had not met death on the bluff? What had happened to his family and friends?

In the gathering darkness, Curly finally made out their trail. And as he followed it, he came upon things which they had dropped in their flight. Suddenly just off the trail he heard the sound of someone weeping. He found a woman crouched in the bushes with a baby in her arms. Sobbing bitterly, she told him that her husband and son had both been killed in the fighting.

"I have only this small papoose," she wailed, "and I am too sick to go on."

"You must go on," Curly said wearily. "You must have care. I saw a broken travois back on the trail. I'll get it."

Before long he was on his way again. And Red Streak was pulling the mended travois bearing the woman and her child. A gray cloud covered the thin moon and rain began to fall. The poor woman sobbed sometimes when the travois poles struck sharp rocks, but the baby was quiet.

[96]

At last the rain stopped. The sky grew
lighter. And just after daybreak, Curly spied
some tepees on the shore of
a little lake not far away. A
moment later, Long Chin
came riding down a near-
by hill.

"I'm guarding the vil-
lage," he said, pulling his
horse up beside
Curly, "so I must
speak quickly.
Have you seen any
signs of whites?"

"Not since I found their trail leading west
at the place of the fight," Curly told him. "Is
my family safe?"

"None was wounded except Spotted Tail,"

[97]

Long Chin replied, "and he will not die, though he was shot four times. Nearly half of our people were killed or captured. Little Thunder and many others were hurt."

Turning, he galloped up the hill to his post. Curly, who was now on foot, led Red Streak toward the tepees.

As he neared the village, his mother came running to meet him with a glad cry because he was safe. Two other women ran up to care for the woman and her baby. And soon Curly was sitting on a pile of sleeping robes, gulping hot soup from a big horn spoon. He was almost too tired to hold his eyes open.

"How did this terrible thing happen?" he asked. "Where is my father?"

"He's caring for some of the wounded," his mother replied. "Now I must feed this papoose, whose family is dead. Little Hawk, begin mending your broken bow. You'll need it if the whites find us. And tell your brother everything that happened."

Little Hawk began wrapping a long leather thong around his bow, talking as he worked.

"It started soon after you and High Shirt left the village. Somebody saw the striped flag coming, and many white soldiers following it.

The women started to pull up the tepee stakes. But Little Thunder said we had nothing to fear, because the whites would not attack a friendly village. Then he and Spotted Tail and Iron Shell went to meet the soldiers, all carrying white peace flags. They smoked a pipe of friendship with the White-Beard Chief and—"

He stopped to find another thong.

"And then—" Curly asked sharply.

"Then Harney, the White Beard, shouted that he had come to get the men who had killed Grattan and his soldiers at the time of the cow trouble."

"But that was long ago!" Curly exclaimed. "And the fight was all mixed up. No one could see even then which Brulés killed the white men."

"That's what our chief told Harney. But White Beard didn't care. Even while he was talking, there were white soldiers hiding near the village. All at once they rushed on us, bringing up their wagon guns. Our men didn't even have weapons ready. But they fought as well as they could while the rest of us got away. Then, when we reached the sand-stone bluff—"

"I know," said Curly quietly.

"They shot down old people and women and children!" Little Hawk exclaimed. "Red Leaf's little girl was captured, and Iron Shell's wife, and Long Chin's mother, and lots of others. Now they must all be in the white-man jail. What will happen to them, Curly?"

"Our people will fight until we get them back," Curly said, in a voice rough with anger. "And we'll avenge the death of every Brulé who's been murdered by the whites."

Curly's words were bravely spoken. And in the days that followed there were many who wanted to fight for the freedom of those who had been captured. But wise Little Thunder, as he was recovering from his wounds, warned his people that they were not strong enough now to send a war party against the fort.

However, the news of Harney's attack on the Brulé village spread rapidly to the other tribes of the Teton Sioux. And the chiefs sent runners to every village to call all the Indians to a great council at Bear Butte near the Black Hills, to decide what must be done about the whites.

CHAPTER TEN

Young Crazy Horse, Warrior

IT WAS a beautiful night. Stars shone brightly over the thousands of tepees which had been set up at Bear Butte near the Black Hills. Campfires leaped high, lighting the huge circle of villages. Drums throbbed steadily. And throughout the whole encampment people were dancing, singing, and feasting.

Curly stood near his father's tepee in the Oglala village, taking great bites of roasted meat from a buffalo rib. When he had finished, he tossed the bone into the fire. As he dragged his hand across his greasy chin, He Dog nudged him with his elbow.

"There goes Sitting Bull," he whispered.

"And Red Cloud himself," Lone Bear mumbled, with his mouth full.

Curly swung around and stared admiringly

at the strong, fine-looking warriors who were striding past. It made the boy's heart swell with pride to see them, and to think of all the other brave men who had met that day in the council lodge. Lone Horn and Touch the Clouds, of the Minniconjous. Little Thunder and Man Afraid. His uncle, Spotted Tail. His best friend, Hump. And many others whose names he did not know.

For five sleeps these leaders of the Teton Sioux had been meeting in the big lodge. To-day they had held their last council, and they had finally decided what must be done about the whites. Curly, sitting just outside the lodge, had listened closely to Red Cloud, who had spoken wisely and well.

"The whites have twice attacked the Brulés," Red Cloud had said gravely. "They have burned a village of our friends, the Cheyennes. And near the Missouri River, they have forced the Indians to stay on little pieces of land called 'reservations' which are jails without walls. More and more whites are crossing the Missouri into our country. We must keep them out of the lands of the Teton Sioux."

"*Hou! Hou!*" The cry had gone up from a thousand throats.

"There are many of us!" Red Cloud had continued in a loud voice. "And we Teton Sioux are strong. We will stick together. We will get guns and powder. Then, except for friendly traders and trappers, we will keep white men forever from these lands!"

Little shivers of excitement ran up Curly's spine at the memory of those stirring words. Then suddenly he realized that Lone Bear was prodding him in the ribs and laughing at him.

"Are you deaf?" Lone Bear asked. "We've told you twice that we're going to join the dancing. Come along."

Curly shook his head. He had never really liked the noisy dances of his people. And he had just caught sight of a lonely figure on a distant hill.

"Go ahead and dance," he said. "I want to talk with my father."

Turning, he sped from the village. Soon father and son were sitting together in silence, looking down on the great encampment. The campfires of the seven large villages twinkled like thousands of glowworms in the night. And the voices of the people rose like the hum of insects in the Moon of Black Cherries.

"I did not know there were so many of us," said Curly, breaking the silence. "Our people are as strong as a great mountain!"

The holy man took his pipe from his mouth and sent a slow puff of smoke toward the sky.

"No people are strong unless they have a strong leader," he remarked wisely. "We have many leaders, but not one who is able to hold us all together. Sometimes, my son, I have hoped that you might become such a leader, but—" He shook his head. "If that were to be so, the great *Wakan Tanka* would have sent you a vision," he added.

"He has," Curly said quietly. And he told his father about the dream which had come to him many moons earlier.

"What did it mean?" he asked.

"It means," replied his father proudly, "that you will grow up to be like the mighty warrior in the dream. You will ride many horses. You will be first in the fighting. But in war you must always dress like the dream warrior. That will be good medicine. Then, as you face the enemy, no bullet or arrow can hurt you. You can be harmed only by someone who attacks you from behind. But you must

[*104*]

always be brave. Braver than any other **man** among our warriors."

"How can a man become brave?" Curly asked quickly.

"A man becomes brave by thinking of others before he thinks of himself," replied the holy man, getting to his feet.

Curly was at his side in an instant. "And if I am as brave as that, will I ever be chosen as a chief?" he asked, eyeing his father anxiously.

The holy man looked long at the starry sky, and then down at the campfires on the plain.

"About becoming a chief," he said slowly, "that I cannot tell. I believe that if you are true to your vision and think often of the good of the people, you will someday be a leader. Perhaps a great leader. But you will need courage and strength. For the way will be hard, my son. The way will be hard."

He pulled his blanket up around his shoulders and they started down the hill. That night Curly went to his sleeping robes, resolving to do many brave deeds, and wondering if he would ever become a chief.

Often in the moons that followed, he pictured himself leading warriors in battle. But it seemed to him as if he would never get a chance to go to war. For the Oglalas had moved to the Powder River country, far north of the white-man road. There were no enemy tribes there. And things were much too peaceful to please Curly and his friends.

Then one morning there was great excitement in the Oglala village. Warriors with brightly painted faces and big feather bonnets were gathering with shield men, who carried shining spears.

"Have the Crows come into this country?" asked Curly, as Hump came riding up to join the war party.

"No," replied Hump, pulling up his big black horse. "We're going against a strange new tribe that has pushed very near to us. They live in grass houses and speak an unknown tongue. Since they seem to have more horses than they need—"

He broke off with a twinkle in his eyes.

"Hump, I want to go," Curly said boldly. "I want to help get those horses. Will you take me along?"

Hump grunted doubtfully. For a long moment he looked down at Curly. The boy was still small for his age. His skin and hair had never been as dark as the skin and hair of most Indians. At first glance, this made him appear weak rather than strong. But he was wiry and tough-muscled, and lately Hump had noticed a new look of determination on his face.

"Get ready, younger brother," Hump said.

Joyfully, Curly turned and sped toward his tepee. When he stepped out a few minutes later he was wearing the blue-stained buckskin leggings his mother had made for him many sleeps before. In his hair was the dried body of a red-backed hawk. A brown pebble hung behind one ear, fastened by a deer-sinew. A yellow zigzag lightning flash was painted on his right cheek and blue hail spots were painted on his chest.

"Now you are a warrior!" cried his mother from the entrance to the tepee, as Curly mounted Red Streak. "Your medicine is good! But be brave, my son. Be brave!"

Curly waved his bow at her and galloped after Hump's men, who were already riding away from the village. They were singing and laughing as they headed west, talking about the coups they would count and the horses they would capture. None of them paid any attention to the boy trailing along behind them.

But this did not bother Curly. He was thinking about his vision.

The grass-house men had been warned that the Oglalas were coming and were waiting on a high hill, hidden behind big rocks. They greeted the Oglalas with a shower of arrows and bullets.

"They have many guns!" Hump shouted to his men. "This will be hard!"

Making high, shrill war cries, the Oglalas circled the hill. Though they managed to shoot some of the grass-house men, they tried in vain to ride to the top. Several of their horses went down, and one Oglala fell, badly wounded. At last they drew up in a half-circle some distance away, wondering if anyone could get up the hill in the face of so much gunfire.

"I can," said Curly. And in an instant he was galloping across the plain at top speed. Straight up the side of the hill he rode, in spite of whining bullets and whizzing arrows. His bowstring twanged as he shot down an enemy warrior who was aiming a gun at him. Then he wheeled quickly and down went another of the enemy. A great shout arose from the Oglalas and Curly's heart was big with pride.

Now he decided that he would do something *really* brave. He slipped from Red Streak's back. Though the enemy were still shooting at him, he quickly scalped both of the dead men.

All at once a grass-house warrior rose from behind a rock just behind Curly and loosed an arrow at him. It hit the boy in the leg. At the same moment there was a sudden burst of firing. Red Streak turned in fright and galloped away before Curly could reach her side.

"Come down! Come down quickly before you're killed!" shouted Hump to Curly as he motioned to his men to circle again in order to draw the enemy's fire.

Limping and in pain, Curly scrambled down the hill, as bullets cut the leaves of the trees around him and arrows glanced from the rocks in his path. Hump was waiting for him on the plain with Red Streak, and they rode out of danger. Then Curly sat down behind a rock while Hump cut the arrowhead from his leg and bandaged the wound with a piece of horse-hide. As Curly watched him, he remembered his vision.

"My father said I could not be hurt except by someone behind me," he told Hump. "And I was hit from behind. That means that everything in my vision will come to pass."

"The medicine of your dream was good," agreed Hump, "for you were not killed. You fought well, younger brother. You are a warrior now, and will need a war horse. We took many fine ponies while you were keeping the enemy busy on the hill. The best one of them all will be yours."

Before Curly could say his thanks, Hump was riding away on his black horse, to round up the rest of the Oglalas. Soon the warriors were on the way home.

The people of the village fell in line behind him

That night there was a victory dance around the blazing campfire. Then each warrior told of a brave deed he had done that day. But when it was Curly's turn, he hung back and said nothing. It was not because his wound was hurting badly. It was because he did not want to stand before many people and make big words about himself.

As he hesitated in the shadows, however, a man began to chant in a deep, strong voice. And everyone grew silent as Curly's father, wrapped in his holy beaded blanket, walked slowly around the circle, singing:

> "Today my son has fought against a
>   strange people,
> He has fought bravely and well.
> He has earned a man's name,
> A good name—a strong name.
> I give up to him the name my father
>   gave up to me.
> From this day he shall be called by
>   the great name—CRAZY HORSE!"

As the holy man sang, the people of the village fell in line behind him, until all were singing and laughing and calling out again and again the name of a brave new warrior:
"Crazy Horse! CRAZY HORSE!"

[*112*]

CHAPTER ELEVEN

"Kill the White Men!"

WHITES coming! Whites coming north. They are following the trail of stakes made by the trapper, Bozeman! Whites coming!"

From scores of hilltops, smoke had risen to the sky in little puffs of gray, signaling this news to all the Teton Sioux. Now hundreds of warriors sat quietly on their horses, surrounding a wagon train in the valley below them. They were just out of range of the white men's guns.

Hump and Red Cloud were the leaders of this large party of warriors. They had decided that there must be no fighting unless the whites began it.

"Don't shoot a bullet or an arrow," they had told the warriors. "Don't shout or move about. When a man must leave the line, another will take his place. At night we will build camp-fires to let the whites know we are still watching them. And in this way we will show them that we will not allow them to cross our lands."

For six days the Sioux had been obeying these orders. And young Crazy Horse had found it harder than any fighting he had ever done since he had become a warrior. He was as restless as his spirited gray horse, which had been captured from the grass-house people four snows earlier. Yet he scarcely moved a muscle as he sat erect in his saddle, staring down at the despairing whites. He felt almost sorry for the pale-skinned people, but he was angry, too.

"We should never have let that trapper, Bozeman, put a line of stakes through our country," he thought. "But who could know he was marking out a road for the whites? Just so they could get to the Big Horn Mountains to dig for that gravel they call gold."

He shifted in his saddle and his war horse tossed her head. Lone Bear, who was beside him, spoke impatiently.

"Why won't Hump let us ride down there and finish off those whites?" he asked. "I want to go home and kill some meat for the winter."

[114]

Crazy Horse smiled. "Hump knows what he's doing," he said. "And so does Red Cloud. He let two whites get through our line last night, just to see where they'd go. They went to the white-man road and sent signals over those new talking wires that the whites have fastened on poles all along the road. Now soldiers are coming from Fort Laramie."

"Soldiers?" Lone Bear repeated. "Well, we're strong enough now to— What's that?"

He fingered his heavy musket as he looked toward the south. Out of a cloud of dust, a Sioux scout came riding hard up the Bozeman Trail. He galloped to a hill where Red Cloud and Hump sat side by side on their horses. Crazy Horse could see him talking to the two leaders. Soon a message had reached all the warriors.

"The soldiers have sent word that they have been ordered to take the whites to Laramie. Move back so that they may come and go in peace. But be prepared for trouble."

Silently the Indians widened their circle around the wagon train. Tensely they watched a company of Blue Coats come riding up the trail. With their bows ready and their guns loaded, they waited for trouble. But none

came. The wagon train, with a line of Blue
Coats riding on either side, started south toward the white-man road. Then a great shout
of triumph went up from the Indians.

"They scurried off like frightened rabbits!" Lone Bear said exultantly as he and Crazy Horse began their long ride home. "And we never even pulled on a bowstring. Now we've really taught the whites that they'd better let us alone."

Crazy Horse nodded. He hoped that Lone Bear was right. There had been no trouble with the whites since White-Beard Harney's attack on the Brulé village. Perhaps that was because many of them had been busy fighting a terrible war among themselves.

Lazy Indians who lived near Fort Laramie

because they liked the soft white-man ways often visited the Sioux camps. These Loaf-About-the-Forts had brought news about this Civil War, and about a new White Father in far-off Washington—a tall chief named Abraham Lincoln. They had talked also about the strange way the whites made war.

"They don't fight in order to get horses as we do," one of the Loafers had told Crazy Horse. "They don't fight even to prove how brave they are by counting coup. They just fight to kill each other."

"I don't care how they fight so long as they keep away from us," Crazy Horse thought now, as he jogged along beside Lone Bear. "And I hope their war lasts longer than the lifetime of an old, old man."

He looked around as He Dog came galloping up, challenging his friends to a race to the foot of a distant hill. In an instant the three young men were off, shouting and whipping up their horses with their coup sticks.

Life was good in the Powder River country in the months that followed the Bozeman Trail affair. There were many buffalo, and there was enough fighting with enemy tribes to provide excitement.

Crazy Horse was rapidly becoming known

as one of the bravest young warriors among the Teton Sioux. He now owned several horses in addition to Red Streak, and a fine new gun which he had captured in a hard-fought battle with some Snakes. With Little Hawk's help he kept his own family and a number of the poor Oglalas well supplied with meat.

One cold day in the Moon of Popping Trees, he and Little Hawk were riding home from a hunt, each with a deer across his pack horse. Their long braids, which hung down over their belted buffalo robes, were covered with frost. And their breath made little clouds of steam as they talked and laughed together.

Suddenly their laughter died away as they rounded the top of a hill and started down toward the village. Usually, on such a cold day as this, the camp was a quiet place, with people staying inside close to the tepee fires. But now it was quite different. Men were making up a large war party. Women were loading pack horses with buffalo robes, sacks of food, and bundles of clothing. And Hump stood near the council lodge, talking excitedly with a group of older warriors.

"What's wrong?" Crazy Horse asked, pulling his horse up beside him.

"It's the white men again," Hump replied

angrily. "Get your war clubs. We're going to ride south to help the Cheyennes."

Crazy Horse and Little Hawk rode quickly

to their tepee. When they entered they found their mother filling a skin sack with *wasna*.

"You may need this on your journey," she said, as she pushed more of the long-keeping hash into the sack. "And if you don't need it, some of the poor Cheyennes will."

"What's happened to them?" Little Hawk asked quickly, as he sat down to pull off his frozen moccasins.

"All those who aren't dead are coming north into our country," his mother replied. "A runner brought the news soon after you left this morning. They were camping on Sand Creek, far south of the Platte, just where the white men had told them to camp. Chief Black Kettle had been all the way to some place called Denver to tell the white chief there that his people were for peace. They'd even given up their weapons, except those they needed for hunting. And then—"

"And then what?" Crazy Horse asked grimly, as he reached for the bag which contained his red-backed hawk and his war paint.

"It was early in the morning," his mother said. "The Cheyennes were sleeping—and a man named Chivington came with white soldiers and—"

Straightening up, she looked at her sons with

tears running down her cheeks. "It was worse than what happened to the Brulés," she went on. "Much worse. Many, many were killed, and scalped, too. Women—children—even papooses. Now you must go to help and—"

"And kill the whites!" Crazy Horse broke in, his face dark with rage.

"My son speaks in a loud voice," said his father, coming into the tepee. "It can be heard as far as the council lodge."

"I will make it heard much farther some day," Crazy Horse cried bitterly. "For the rest of my life I shall hate all white men!"

Gathering up his weapons, Crazy Horse strode from the tepee. When the warriors set out some time later, he was still angry.

They traveled rapidly, leaving the older men to bring on the loaded pack horses. Meanwhile the news of the massacre at Sand Creek was spreading as swiftly as a forest fire. Soon warriors from other tribes were riding hard toward the south. Minniconjous, Brulés, and No Bows. Blackfeet, fierce Hunkpapas, and northern Cheyennes. In the minds of all of them was one thought—revenge.

CHAPTER TWELVE

On the Warpath

As THE Sioux rode rapidly south, the Cheyennes were pushing north. Hundreds of Indians from other tribes had joined them. For they had decided after the Cheyenne massacre that they could never trust the white men again. Now, nearly six thousand Indians, with their tepees, dogs, and horses, were traveling together toward the Powder River country.

Because of the wounded and the women and children, they moved slowly. Indeed, they had not yet reached the ice-covered Platte when they were met by the Oglala warriors and some of the other Sioux. That night they all camped in the hills near the river.

It was a clear night in January, the Moon of Frost on the Tepee. A cold wind was blowing. Hump belted his buffalo robe more tightly around his waist as he stepped from the council lodge. Pulling his warm hood over his head, he strode toward the edge of the great encampment. There the Oglala warriors were waiting for him, near a blazing fire.

"I've been talking with one of the Cheyenne chiefs," he said. "Tomorrow the people will stay here while a war party attacks a white-man fort at a place called Julesburg. Seven warriors will be needed as decoys to lure the soldiers from the fort. Five of the decoys will be Cheyennes, and two will be Sioux."

"I want to be one of them!" Crazy Horse called quickly.

"Hou!" replied Hump. "You will be one and I will be the other. The rest of you warriors will hide with the Cheyennes in the sand hills, some distance from the fort. You must stay out of sight until we decoys have fooled the soldiers into following us right up to a place where you can surround them. Then—"

"Then death to the white men!" shouted He Dog, as he leaped to his feet.

All the warriors began talking eagerly about the coming attack. All except Crazy Horse. He sat silent and thoughtful. He had acted as a decoy before, in war parties against the

Crows to get horses. This war party would be different. For the first time in his life he was going against the white soldiers. And he was going against them to get scalps.

As he looked up at the cold stars, thinking out the tricks he would use to lure the white men into ambush, he heard the quiet voice of Hump.

"Get to your sleeping robes, all of you! We're starting at daybreak!"

In the gray light of early dawn, the war party made ready to leave. A thousand warriors painted their faces. Some armed themselves with shields, lances, and war clubs. Others with bows and arrows. A few had guns. Mounting their horses, they fell into line.

The chiefs in their big feathered war bonnets galloped up to lead the procession. Scouts were sent ahead. And the long column began to move toward Julesburg, over broken hills covered with sagebrush and soapweed.

Crazy Horse, with a yellow lightning mark on one cheek and a red-backed hawk in his hair, rode beside Hump.

A pale sun rose and began its slow walk up the sky. Before it had climbed far, the warriors were well hidden in the sand hills, two miles from Julesburg. And the decoys were riding through a narrow ravine which ran close to the fort.

Meanwhile the people in the little frontier town of Julesburg were going about their business as usual. Just outside the fort, near the edge of the town, several men were chopping up firewood. Suddenly seven painted warriors came riding out of the ravine near by and charged straight at them. Yelling with terror, the men ran into the fort and pushed the gates shut.

The Indians laughed as though they had been playing a joke. Turning their horses, they rode off toward the sand hills until they were out of gunshot. As they had hoped it would, a bugle sounded shrilly inside the fort. The gates were thrown open and more than sixty troopers came riding out.

Crazy Horse and the other decoys whipped up their horses, yet at the same time they held them back so that the troopers could gain on them. But just when the soldiers were almost within gunshot, the Indians spurted ahead.

For a moment it looked as if the soldiers would give up the chase. Suddenly Crazy

[126]

Horse stopped his pony, dismounted, and stooped over to look at her leg, pretending she was hurt. In a burst of speed several troopers galloped toward him, leveling their guns. As a bullet whistled past his head, he sprang to his saddle and rode on, the Blue Coats after him.

Quickly the other decoys turned and sent arrows flying at the oncoming soldiers, taking care not to hit any of them. Then, shouting warnings at each other, they galloped ahead, looking back over their shoulders now and then as if they were terrified. Nearer and nearer they led the troopers to the hills where the warriors were hiding.

"Come on," Hump shouted as Crazy Horse fell behind again to send an arrow toward the troopers. "They're all following us now and we've almost got them where we want them."

Crazy Horse whipped up his pony. "A little farther and every Blue Coat will be wiped out!" he cried exultantly. "If only the warriors will wait till—"

He never finished his sentence. At that moment a young Cheyenne rose from behind a hill and fired an old gun at the Blue Coats. As if that were their signal, a score of impatient young warriors broke out of hiding. Shooting and making shrill war cries, they raced toward the troopers. Hundreds of other warriors followed, all eager to count coup on the whites.

Three of the Blue Coats fell from their saddles. The rest wheeled and fled for the fort at top speed, with the Indians in hot pursuit. Before the troopers were safely inside the gate they had lost fifteen more men.

Yelling with disappointment and shouting wild threats, some of the warriors rode around and around the fort. Others galloped through Julesburg looking for whites. But everybody in town had already taken refuge behind the fort's stout walls.

"If we can't kill whites, we can wreck their village as they wrecked the villages of the Brulés and Cheyennes!" Crazy Horse cried loudly. "And we'll tear down all the talking wires so that they can't signal for more soldiers!"

In no time at all, he and a band of young braves were pulling up the slender poles of the telegraph line. Other Indians had begun to round up all the horses in town, and to break into stores and warehouses. Pushing into these buildings, some of the warriors brought out sacks of sugar and flour and coffee; bundles of blankets and clothing; and bolts of cloth.

Mounting their war ponies, they galloped across the prairie, unrolling the cloth as they went, and laughing to see the bright streamers floating out behind them. Then He Dog and Lone Bear rode after them, letting the wind take handfuls of the twenty-dollar bills which they had found in an iron money box.

By the time the sun had reached the middle of the sky, a long column of Indians was moving over the hills from Julesburg. And smoke was rising high from several buildings which they had set afire.

That night some of the Sioux sat around

their campfire, boasting about the coups they had counted and the horses they had captured.

"It was a good war party," He Dog remarked, looking very funny in a too-small soldier coat he had taken from a warehouse. "Don't you think so, Crazy Horse?"

"I thought so while it was going on," Crazy Horse replied soberly. "But we killed only eighteen whites, He Dog. And we could have killed them all if everybody had obeyed orders."

His voice grew louder. "We'll never beat the whites," he cried, "unless we fight together for the good of all, instead of—"

He broke off suddenly. For he had just realized that everyone was listening to him. And it still made him feel uncomfortable to speak before many people. That night he said nothing more about the way the Indians waged war. But as time passed, he thought about it a great deal. And one day nearly seven moons later, he spoke of it again.

The six thousand Indians from the south had reached the Powder River country safely. Many Loafers from Fort Laramie had joined them, and even some white men who were married to Indian women. As they had moved through the country near the Platte, many little war parties had harried the whites, burning cabins and ranch houses, attacking stagecoaches and wagon trains, and taking scalps. No large war party had been sent out, however, since the attack on Julesburg.

Now it was July, the Moon When Cherries Are Ripe. And a thousand warriors had ridden south from the Powder River country to attack a strong fort at Platte Bridge. Again Crazy Horse was one of the decoys. With three others, he rode close to the fort. Trying every trick they knew, the brave decoys lured the soldiers from the fort and almost to the hills where the warriors were hiding in ambush.

Then, just as they had at Julesburg, a few of the young warriors rushed into the open, firing wildly. Wheeling their horses, the soldiers rode swiftly back to the fort. And not a man was killed.

Crazy Horse was furious.

"Are you papooses?" he shouted later to a group of warriors which had gathered on a hill. "Can't you wait until you get the signal to attack? Because you each want to count coup, you disobey the leaders and spoil our ambush! We'll never defeat the white men until every warrior learns to fight for the people and not for himself! Never!"

He turned as someone stepped up beside him. It was the great chief, Man Afraid. His face was grave.

"The brave son of our holy man has spoken wisely," he told the warriors in a loud voice. "After one more sleep, we will try again to trap and kill the soldiers from the Platte Bridge fort. We will hide in the brush near the bridge. The Cheyennes will hide in the hills. And while you young warriors are waiting for your signal to attack, remember the words of Crazy Horse."

"*Hou!*" agreed Lone Bear, Little Hawk, and many others, feeling sorry and ashamed. But some of the warriors turned away, grumbling. What glory was there in fighting if they couldn't rush out and count coup?

The next morning the decoys rode again toward the fort. They pretended that they were going to stampede a large herd of horses, but were afraid to begin. Soon the fort gates opened and soldiers came galloping out. As Crazy Horse rode away from them, he glanced anxiously at the brush where the Sioux were hiding. Would the warriors wait until the trap could be sprung on the soldiers? Would they? They did!

That night war drums throbbed as the warriors shuffled around their campfire in a dance of victory. And when they started north next day, they took with them guns, bullets, horses, mules, and many white-man scalps.

Young Crazy Horse rode beside He Dog.

"Now at last we're learning to work together," he said proudly. "And the Cheyennes have been avenged."

CHAPTER THIRTEEN

The Shirt Wearer

IT WAS a beautiful day in April, the Moon of Grass Appearing. The sky was clear, and the sun was warm. But in spite of the fine weather, the old camp crier had pains in his joints. He walked slowly as he made his rounds through the Oglala village.

"Co-o! Co-o!" he called. "Come out, people. This is the day the Big Bellies will name the four Shirt Wearers. This is the day the old chiefs are going to name four brave young men to be leaders. Co-o! Co-o! Come out."

At once the people began to gather before their tepees, for they were all eager to know whom the chiefs would choose for helpers.

"You'll be chosen—wait and see!" said Little Hawk to his brother.

Crazy Horse shook his head. "No," he said. "The chiefs will choose their sons. And I've done nothing to deserve—"

"Look!" Little Hawk broke in. "Here come the Tellers of Names."

Two men dressed in brightly painted robes had begun to ride slowly around the village circle. As they approached Crazy Horse, the young warrior's heart pounded wildly. In spite of what he had just said, he had a faint hope that he might be chosen. But the Tellers passed him by and stopped before Young Man Afraid. The women made a polite trilling sound as the son of the head chief stepped forward.

The Tellers rode around a second time, and the women trilled again when they stopped before the son of good Chief Brave Bear. Once more the Tellers circled, and the son of Chief Sitting Bear stepped forward. Then they started around for the last time.

"Now they'll choose the son of that old Big Belly, Chief Bad Face," thought Crazy Horse. But a moment later he caught his breath. The Tellers had stopped before *him!*

There was no polite trilling as he stepped forward. He had not been chosen because he was a chief's son, but because he was brave and wise. And the people shouted for joy.

"Crazy Horse! Crazy Horse! Crazy Horse!"

Then the four young men were mounted on fine horses and led to the council lodge. There the Big Bellies welcomed them and each man was given a beaded shirt. On each shirt were pictures of the brave deeds which had been done by the man who was to wear it.

"There are more pictures on our son's shirt than on any other," the mother of Crazy Horse whispered proudly to her husband.

The holy man nodded but did not reply, for already an old, old chief had begun to speak to the four young men.

"My sons," the old chief said in a thin, high voice, "you have been chosen to help us lead our people. You will lead them in camp, on the hunt, and at war. Care for the poor and the helpless. Be generous, wise, and firm. Meet your enemies strongly and bravely. You are now Shirt Wearers!"

A great cheering went up from the crowd when he had finished. And Crazy Horse did not know which way to turn his eyes, with so many people looking at him. But he was happier than he had been since the day he had won his man-name.

Late that night when the feasting and dancing were over he walked alone to the top of a little hill. There, looking up at the stars, he prayed to *Wakan Tanka* to help him become a truly great leader.

It was not long before he had a chance to prove that he was a wise, brave leader. For again there was trouble on the Bozeman

Trail. Since it was the shortest route north to the Montana Territory, where gold had been discovered, the white men were determined to use it. But those who tried to travel on it were attacked or driven back by small parties of warriors.

At last the United States Government tried to buy the trail. Messages were sent to some of the Sioux chiefs, offering them many presents if they would come to Fort Laramie to discuss the matter. Man Afraid and Red Cloud both went to the meeting. It was June, the Moon of Making Fat, when they returned. That evening the Oglalas crowded around the council lodge to hear their report. Man Afraid spoke first.

"We were promised that our people would get wagonloads of presents from the new White Father in Washington, if we would sell the trail," he said.

"But those were crooked words," Red Cloud added in a loud voice. "Already the White Father had sent soldiers to steal the trail. We saw them marching toward it, even while we were talking to the white men. And later we heard from a Loafer that the soldiers were going up the trail to build a fort where Piney Creek runs into the Powder River."

"We must stop them before they begin the fort!" Crazy Horse cried, jumping to his feet.

Man Afraid shook his head. He was old and tired and discouraged.

"No," he said slowly, "we cannot send out a big war party now. This is the time to make meat for the people and to have our summer sun dance. Is that not so, Red Cloud?"

"*Hou!*" agreed Red Cloud.

Crazy Horse tried to hide his anger and disappointment. "These men may be great leaders," he thought, "but they close their eyes at the wrong time. Something must be done *now.*"

When the council ended, he gathered a group of young warriors around him and told them that he would lead them down to Piney Creek.

"We cannot make a real attack on the white men, for there are not enough of us," he said. "But we can make them wish they had never come into our country."

So it was that the soldiers who were building the fort on Piney Creek found themselves harassed, day after day, by small groups of Indians. Woodcutters who were felling logs in the forest a few miles from the fort were often attacked. Blue Coats who left the fort to get water sometimes failed to return. Horses and cattle disappeared. Sentries were shot from ambush. Yet the soldiers kept bravely on with their work. In October they completed the fort and named it Fort Kearny.

By that time many warriors had ridden down from the Oglalas' camp in the Black Hills, to join Crazy Horse. And Red Cloud had at last sent out a war pipe to call fighting men from every Sioux and Cheyenne village to come to Piney Creek.

CHAPTER FOURTEEN

The Fight at Fort Kearny

I T WAS December, the Moon of Popping Trees, before the Indians were ready to make a big attack on the soldiers at Fort Kearny. Hump and Crazy Horse carefully planned it together. On the night before the attack, Hump spoke in strong words to the Sioux warriors.

"We do not have far-shooting guns like the white soldiers," he said. "And we have few bullets for the guns we do have. So we must decoy the Blue Coats from the fort and trap them, as we trapped the soldiers at Platte Bridge. The most dangerous work will be done by the man who leads the decoys. That man will be our brave young Shirt Wearer, Crazy Horse."

The warriors grunted approvingly, and

Crazy Horse stepped up to speak to them.

"You know about the white chief, Fetterman," he said. "He is the man who makes big words about how weak we are. 'Give me eighty men,' he says, 'and I will ride through the whole Sioux nation.' Let us show him tomorrow how far he will get."

"*Hou!*" shouted the warriors. "*Hou!*"

"This is our plan," Crazy Horse went on quickly. "Tomorrow a party of Cheyennes will attack the woodcutters when they are at work in the forest. The woodcutters will make their signal for help—five shots. When the soldiers come out of the fort to ride to their rescue, we decoys will be waiting.

"We'll lead the Blue Coats north over Lodge Trail Ridge. You warriors will be hiding on the other side of the ridge, behind hills and in ravines. If you wait until I wave my blanket over my head as a signal to attack, we can trap them all. If you don't wait—"

"We will wait!" shouted many of the warriors. And the others cried, "*Hou! Hou!*"

Before it was light next morning, the big war party rode down along the ice-covered Piney. Above the fort, many of the Cheyennes turned off toward the forest. Before long all the remaining warriors except the decoys were well hidden on the north side of Lodge Trail Ridge. The ten mounted decoys then approached the fort through the brush, taking care that they should not be seen. Soon, from their hiding places, they saw the woodcutters leave the fort and ride toward the forest.

Snow had fallen during the night. Now the sky was clear, but the wind was bitter cold. Crazy Horse pulled his thick blanket around his shoulders and settled himself in the saddle. For a long time he sat motionless, thinking of the fighting to be done that day, and waiting for the signal which meant that the woodcutters had been attacked.

Suddenly there came the welcome sound of five shots from the forest. A moment later the shrill notes of a bugle were heard from the fort.

"Come," said Crazy Horse quietly to the other decoys. "It is time."

The gates of the fort were opened. Just as the soldiers rode out, the decoys let themselves be seen. Calling out excitedly, some of the Blue Coats pointed at the Indians. Fetterman, who was leading, shouted a command. The frozen earth around the decoys was sprayed with bullets. But none of the Indians was hit. Yelling as though they were in fear of their lives, they galloped toward Lodge Trail Ridge, with Crazy Horse last, to protect the rear.

The soldiers rode after them, shooting. Near the top of the ridge, Crazy Horse looked back. There were too many soldiers to count, but it seemed as if Fetterman must have more than his eighty men!

Before they had reached the foot of the ridge, Fetterman pulled up his horse and called out sharply. The soldiers stopped. Crazy Horse watched in dismay. Were they going to turn back so soon? Had Fetterman guessed that he and his men might be trapped? Or had he decided that so few Indians weren't worth chasing?

"A boasting man's pride is easily hurt," Crazy Horse said to himself. "And he loses his head if he's angered. Now is the time for the blanket trick."

He shouted to two of the decoys. "He Dog! Lone Bear! Your blankets!"

Snatching up blankets which lay folded across their saddles, the two decoys galloped down the ridge after Crazy Horse, who was already charging at the soldiers. Whooping wildly, the three Oglalas waved their blankets, frightening the soldiers' horses and angering the Blue Coats.

In a loud voice Fetterman commanded his men to ride the Indians down. As the Blue Coats started for the decoys, the Indians quickly turned their horses and fled up the high rocky ridge. On came the soldiers, up and over the top.

[*145*]

Now the heart of Crazy Horse was pounding as hard as the hoofs of his war pony. Back and forth he galloped, shouting at the white soldiers, and waiting for the moment when the last soldier had entered the trap. Then all at once he whirled his blanket over his head.

"Hoka hey!" His voice rang out. *"Hoppo!* Let's go!"

In an instant the country was alive with yelling, shooting Indians. Wheeling around, the white troops started back up the ridge, fighting as they went. The air was thick with bullets and arrows. Horses screamed with pain or fright. Men groaned. Warriors made shrill war cries. Rifles cracked. And smoke lay thick above the reddening snow.

Crazy Horse, with his red-backed hawk in his hair, seemed to be everywhere at once. Directing the fighting. Shouting encouragement to the other warriors. Knocking down white soldiers with his war club. And, finally, blazing away with a new rifle which he pulled from the hands of a dying Blue Coat. The battle was a bitter one. By the time it ended, twelve Indians had been killed and Fetterman with all his men lay dead.

Crazy Horse had proved himself a wise

[146]

leader. And already he was thinking about an attack against the soldiers who still remained in the fort. But even while the Indians were carrying their wounded back to camp, a howling blizzard swept down from the north. There was no more fighting that winter. For three moons, the Powder River country was deep in snow.

With the coming of warm weather, however, the fighting began again. Crazy Horse, Hump, and Sitting Bull all led many war parties against the enemy. Ranches were burned. Wagon trains were attacked. Horses and cattle were stolen. And few white persons were safe on the Bozeman Trail, or on the white-man road near the Platte.

At last, one day in July, a Loafer from Fort Laramie rode into the big Oglala camp on Tongue River. Crazy Horse, who had just returned from a raid, hurried to the council lodge to see what news he had brought. The people had already gathered there, and the Loafer began to speak.

"The white men have many presents at the fort for all of you," he announced. "Blankets, knives, axes, kettles, tobacco—and even guns and bullets. All will be yours if you will stop fighting the white men and if your chiefs will sign a peace paper."

"Tell the white men we don't want their presents!" Crazy Horse shouted angrily. "Tell them that we will give them no peace until they get out of our country and stay out. Tell them that we won't even talk about peace until all the Blue Coats have left Fort Kearny and marched back to Fort Laramie."

"*Hoye!*" cried the people, feeling proud because they had such a strong leader. "*Hou! Hoye!*"

Back to the fort rode the Loafer with the message from Crazy Horse. And soon afterward another messenger arrived at the fort. He had been to see Sitting Bull, who was camping with his people on the Yellowstone River just north of the Powder. That brave leader had also refused to talk about peace until the Blue Coats had left the Powder River country. And so at last the United States Government decided to give up Fort Kearny.

On a hot August morning Crazy Horse, Hump, Red Cloud, and hundreds of other Indians sat proudly on their horses, watching a Blue Coat haul down the striped flag over the fort. Then, in a long column, the soldiers rode out of Fort Kearny and slowly moved south down the Bozeman Trail.

The Indians had won a great victory. At last they had driven the white men from their

land. Shouting with joy, they set fire to the hated fort and the high stockade. By the time the sun had left the sky, there was nothing left of Fort Kearny but ashes and smoke.

It was not long after this that the Indians

[*149*]

decided they must have a treaty chief. Since Red Cloud was a man of big words, they chose him to deal with the white leaders and sent him to Fort Laramie to put his mark on the peace paper. When he came back he told the Indians that the white men had agreed to keep out of the Powder River country forever.

"They have promised that the land shall be ours as long as grass shall grow and water flow," he said.

"The land always was ours," thought Crazy Horse. "But that's a good promise. I wonder how long the white men will keep it."

They kept their promise for six years! Then gold was discovered in the Black Hills. Miners with picks, shovels, and pack horses swarmed into the Powder River country, frightening away the buffalo with their noise. Soldiers went along to protect the miners. And the White Father sent word to the Sioux that he wished to buy the Black Hills for his people.

Crazy Horse, Sitting Bull, and other strong leaders refused to sell the land which the good *Wakan Tanka* had given them. But there were two leaders who were willing to sell the hills if they could get a big enough price. One was Red Cloud. The other was Spotted Tail.

Something had happened to those two chiefs which Crazy Horse could not understand. Once they had both been brave warriors. But soon after the peace paper was signed, they had been invited to Washington to meet the White Father.

When they returned, loaded with gifts, they had reported that they had seen more white men than there were stars in the sky. Then they had announced that they had each been given a reservation not far from Fort Laramie. Now they were living on these reservations with many of their people.

Crazy Horse was disgusted with the two chiefs and with all who had gone with them.

"Their hearts have turned to water because they fear the whites," he thought scornfully. "They are like the lazy Loafers, growing soft and fat on white-man food."

It was a snowy evening and he was riding home, leading a string of pack horses which he had taken in a hard fight with some miners. He was eager to reach his tepee, for he was married now. And he knew that his young wife, Black Shawl, was waiting for him with a good fire blazing and buffalo stew bubbling in the big iron pot.

Yanking on the lead rope, he hurried on toward the village. But even before he reached there, He Dog and Little Big Man came riding out to meet him.

"We've waited long for you," said He Dog, pulling up his horse. "A Loafer is here with a message from Fort Laramie. It is a bad thing, Crazy Horse. The white men are still very angry because we won't sell the Black Hills. Now they say that all Indians in the Powder River country must move to reservations before another moon has grown fat."

"And if we refuse to move?" asked Crazy Horse in a quiet voice. "What then?"

"Then the White Father will send a great army against us," said Little Big Man. "What do you say, Crazy Horse? What shall we do?"

"Stay in our own country," Crazy Horse replied firmly. "We'll join forces with Sitting Bull and when the soldiers come, we'll be ready for them. If the white men want war, my friends, they shall have it. And this time it will be war to the end."

CHAPTER FIFTEEN

The New War Chief

THE breeze which blew down the valley of the Rosebud was filled with the scent of spring flowers. Along the river, the children shouted at their play. But there was hardly a sound in the big council lodge, although it was filled with people.

The mother of Crazy Horse tugged at the sleeve of the woman beside her.

"My eyes are getting so old I can't see, Black Shawl," she whispered. "Who is there in the center of the lodge besides my son?"

Black Shawl studied the chiefs who were seated in a half-circle around Crazy Horse.

"Sitting Bull is there," she said softly, "and Two Moons of the Cheyennes, and Touch the Clouds of the Minniconjous, and—"

"Hush!" commanded a woman who stood

near her. "Big Road of the Oglalas is standing up to speak."

In a moment the voice of Big Road rang out through the council lodge. Even the people crowded outside the lodge could hear every word.

"My friends," said Big Road, "more than four moons have passed since the white men made loud talk about sending an army against us. Now at last the soldiers are on their way and we must be ready for a hard fight. We need a strong chief to lead us.

"Today we Oglalas have chosen such a chief. We have chosen a brave man who has led our warriors against many enemies. A wise, generous man who will be a good father to the people. A great man who will be our war chief as long as he lives. His name is Crazy Horse!"

"Crazy Horse! Crazy Horse!"

The people cheered so joyfully that Black Shawl could hardly contain her pride. With shining eyes, she watched her husband take the long feathered pipe which was handed to him and puff on it solemnly. Next he was lifted up and carried outside the lodge. There he was mounted on a big prancing white war horse. Finally, with the chiefs and all the cheering people following him, Crazy Horse rode slowly around the great encampment.

He was proud that he had been made a war chief, but he was worried, too. It was a heavy responsibility. Hundreds of Oglalas, Hunkpapas, Minniconjous, No Bows, and Chey-

ennes had banded together to fight the white men. And all the warriors would look to him for leadership.

That evening when the chief-making ceremony was over, Crazy Horse went alone to a hilltop. Raising his hands toward the sky, he prayed to *Wakan Tanka* for help in leading and protecting his people.

Meanwhile Oglala messengers were hurrying south to the reservations of Spotted Tail and Red Cloud.

"We must make a big fight to hold our country," they told the reservation Indians. "Crazy Horse is our war chief now. He will lead us. Come and help!"

As soon as they heard this news, many warriors gathered up their weapons and told their wives to get ready to move. Some families stole away from the reservations after dark. Others left boldly in the broad daylight. And all headed north for the great encampment on the Rosebud River.

One of these reservation Indians was a cousin to Crazy Horse—an old lame warrior named Black Elk. As soon as Black Elk reached the Oglala village he went to the war chief's home.

"I thought I'd find you in a bigger tepee," he said to Crazy Horse. "One which is finely decorated and worthy of a great war chief."

Crazy Horse laughed. "I've never liked showy things," he said. "Now sit down, my friend, and while Black Shawl fixes you some food, tell me what news you've learned on your way north."

Black Elk lowered himself to the ground with a weary sigh.

"One thing I learned is this," he said, settling himself comfortably against a back rest. "The soldier-chief, Crook, is camping on Goose Creek. He has more Blue Coats with him than ants in an anthill. And he's bribing Crows to scout for him and to help him fight."

"That's not news," Crazy Horse said with a smile. "I myself have spied out Crook's camp and seen his soldiers and his Indian scouts. Tell me something else."

"Long Hair, the soldier-chief the white men call Custer, is coming from the east with more soldiers," Black Elk replied.

Crazy Horse nodded. "I know that, too," he said. "And they're all well armed. But we'll be ready for them."

He reached up to take the big horn spoon full of stew from Black Shawl and handed it to his cousin. As the old man ate, the two cousins talked sadly about Little Hawk, who had been killed by some white men while he was hunting. And about Hump, who had fallen in a battle with the Snakes. At last the old man left to go to his own tepee which his wife had set up at the edge of the village.

[157]

Shortly after this visit, all the Indians in the great encampment moved west to Ash Creek, for scouts had reported a small herd of buffalo near by. Before long the people were making meat and enjoying themselves as they always did when they were all together.

Only their leaders seemed to think of the danger which threatened them all. Both Crazy Horse and Sitting Bull kept scouts out day and night, roaming the hills and valleys in every direction, looking for some signs of the enemy.

On a warm evening in June, the Moon of Making Fat, Crazy Horse stood outside his tepee, talking with his old father. Suddenly he stopped speaking and listened intently. He thought he had heard a wolf howl in the distance. Yes, there it was again, closer this time. One of the scouts was riding in, signaling danger.

Quickly Crazy Horse untied a pony which was tethered near his tepee and rode out to meet him. When the two men returned, the war chief sent runners to all the villages in the encampment to tell the people to come at once to the council lodge.

Soon the big lodge was filled and sur-

rounded by excited men, women, and children. In the center, which was lighted by a
flickering fire, the chiefs sat down in a circle
to hear the scout's report.

"Soldiers are coming," the scout announced
in a loud voice. "Many soldiers! They come
with the white chief called Crook from Goose
Creek. The Rosebud is black with them!"

"The Rosebud!" A frightened murmur ran
through the crowd. The Rosebud River was
less than one sleep away.

[*159*]

Two of the women started to cry and everyone else began to talk excitedly. Then Crazy Horse rose to his feet.

"My friends," he called in a loud voice, "this is no time for foolish words. Let us plan."

He stopped speaking and the crowd grew quiet to hear what else he would say.

"The old chiefs and their warriors will stay here to protect the helpless ones," he went on. "And a big war party will leave at once to fight the soldiers on the Rosebud. I will lead it and all who are truly brave will follow me."

"*Hoye!*" shouted the warriors. "*Hou! Hou!*"

Crazy Horse held up his hand for silence.

"Think well before you call '*Hoye!*'" he said. "The whites are very, very strong. For some of you this will be a new kind of fighting. It must not be a fighting to count coup and to do brave deeds to be told later around the fire. It must be a fighting all together. We must fight to kill! We must fight to the end so that we can live in peace in our own country."

"*Hou!*" shouted the warriors again. "*Hoye!*"

"Then let us go," commanded Crazy Horse.

CHAPTER SIXTEEN

The Greatest Victory

THE meeting broke up and the warriors scattered to get their weapons. When Crazy Horse reached his tepee, Black Shawl was waiting with his two war horses and a fringed bag containing his war clothes. For an instant he held her close to him. And then he was gone.

Drums throbbed and the women sang strong-heart songs as the men rode away into the dark night. It was daylight when the warriors stopped near the Rosebud to rest their horses and to eat a little *wasna*.

Crazy Horse walked around among them, commanding some to fight on one side of the river and some on the other. Then he fastened his red-backed hawk in his hair, and painted the lightning mark on his cheek. After tying a cape of spotted red calfskin around his shoulders, he mounted his big white charger.

"Hoppo!" he said to the braves who were nearest him. "Let us go."

A long ridge ran parallel to the Rosebud between the warriors and the river. As they topped this ridge the Sioux saw that the valley below them was filled with soldiers. At that moment there was a cry from some of Crook's Indian scouts.

"Sioux coming!" they shouted, running into Crook's camp. "Sioux coming! Heap Sioux!"

Almost immediately a bugle sounded shrilly. Blue Coats grabbed their guns, ran for their horses, and wheeled into battle line. Obeying a sharp command, some of them fired at the oncoming Sioux and the fight was on.

All day it raged, up and down the ridges and bluffs, over the broad valley. At first the Indians seemed to be winning. Then the whites began to drive them back with their many far-shooting guns.

Suddenly Crazy Horse saw that some of his men were retreating, whipping up their horses to get out of the enemy's range.

[*162*]

"Be strong!" he shouted. "Remember the weak and helpless ones at home! Brave hearts follow me! Cowards to the rear! *Hoka hey!* This is a good day to die!" Waving his rifle, he rode boldly toward the advancing soldiers.

"*Hoka hey!*" yelled He Dog, wheeling his

horse around. And others roared, "*Hoka hey!*" as they turned and galloped into the fray again.

Now the Blue Coats began to fall back, hard-pressed on three sides by fiercely fighting warriors. At last there was a blare of bugles. The whites were retreating! By the time the sun had walked down the sky, they were moving along the river, toward their camp on Goose Creek.

The Indians did not pursue them, for they had used all of their ammunition and most of their arrows. Eight of the Sioux had been killed and some had been wounded, but Crazy Horse knew that Crook's losses were far greater.

It had been a hard fight and Crazy Horse had won his greatest victory. Yet he and his warriors were almost too tired to rejoice. By daybreak they had returned to the big encampment. And the following morning, Sitting Bull, who was the leader of all the Teton Sioux, sent out criers to tell the people that they must get ready to move to the Little Big Horn River.

This was a fine place for an encampment. Soon the village circles were strung out along the river for three miles. There was plenty of good grass for the horses. There were buffalo to the west. And everyone was glad to be farther away from the whites.

That night there was dancing and singing in every village, and the next morning there was much visiting back and forth. Boys splashed in the cool, clear waters of the river.

Groups of women went out to dig wild turnips in the hills. Warriors sat about discussing the fight on the Rosebud and the great victory of their chief, Crazy Horse, over the white general, Crook.

"If Crazy Horse had not taught us to fight together," said Red Fox, "we could never have driven back the whites. But he is a strange chief. He gives away everything he owns to the poor, except what he needs for war. He does not wish to be praised and—"

"Here he comes!" broke in Big Eagle.

Respectfully they eyed their chief as he strode past them and mounted the pony before his tepee. Seeing that all was well with his people for the time being, Crazy Horse then set out to visit a friend in the Cheyenne village which was farthest down the river.

It was a warm June day and the two friends sat outside, talking of many things. Suddenly they heard shots and at the same time a runner came pounding into the village.

"Soldiers! Soldiers!" he yelled. "Upriver. South of the Hunkpapas!"

Springing to his saddle, Crazy Horse galloped toward the Hunkpapa village. In every village there was now great noise and confusion. Women were crying, calling for their children, snatching up their papooses and hurrying away from the encampment. Boys were yelling as they drove the horses thundering down from the hills. Leaders were blowing their shrill eagle-bone whistles to summon their warriors. Sitting Bull, Two Moons, and all the other chiefs were shouting orders.

As fast as a warrior caught a horse, he rode off whooping to the fight. It was a desperate battle, for the Sioux were determined that the white soldiers should not enter their villages. At last they succeeded in driving the soldiers across the Little Big Horn, killing many. The rest took refuge on a hill. Then the Indians started to encircle them. But at that moment there came another cry of alarm.

"More soldiers coming! Many more! Horse-soldiers! Downriver, across from the Minniconjous!"

"*Hoppo!*" shouted Crazy Horse to his warriors. "Be brave, my friends. Fight together. Remember the earth is all that lasts! Be strong and follow me!"

Holding his rifle high over his head, he galloped down along the river, with the warriors behind him, whipping up their horses and making their shrill war cries. Sitting Bull, too, was leading warriors down along the river. Soon over two hundred well-armed Blue Coats were surrounded by Indians, and all were fighting for their lives. They fought courageously. But when the battle was over, every one of them was dead.

Now the young warriors went wild. Yelling with triumph, they began to strip the dead bodies, pulling off uniforms and shoes, and yanking rings from the fingers of the whites.

Crazy Horse watched them, shaking his head. He did not want them to do this, but he did not try to stop them. For they had fought well, remembering all that he had taught them. Suddenly he heard shooting to the south, and knew that some of his braves must be trying to finish off the soldiers who had taken refuge on the hill.

He rode off swiftly to help them. But by this time the Blue Coats were firmly entrenched. Though the warriors fought until dark they could not dislodge them.

Many Indians had been killed in the fighting that day, and there was wailing and mourning all through the encampment that night, as the Sioux buried their dead. Early the next morning, scouts signaled that more soldiers were coming with cannon. Hastily the Indians packed their travois, rounded up their horses, and moved north, setting the grass afire before they left.

Most of them did not yet know the name of the man who had directed the Blue Coats in their second big fight. But Crazy Horse had learned it and so had Sitting Bull.

That night, when the camp had been made

and the people were resting, the two great chiefs discussed the matter, as they sat outside Sitting Bull's tepee.

"So it was Long Hair who led the Blue Coats in that last big fight," Crazy Horse remarked, in a low voice.

"*Hou!*" grunted Sitting Bull, stuffing some tobacco into the bowl of his long-stemmed pipe. "It was the chief the white men call Custer. He was a brave man."

"Yes, he was brave," Crazy Horse agreed. Then he added thoughtfully, "Do you know, my friend, that we have never before killed as many Blue Coats as we did yesterday on the

[*169*]

Little Big Horn? And my heart should feel good. But there is something black about our victory. Something very black."

Sitting Bull said nothing. He, too, was heavy-hearted and worried about the future. Although the Indians had taken many guns in their two big fights, they had little ammunition.

"And we cannot fight white men forever," he thought. "We must hunt or we will starve."

For some time the two chiefs sat smoking in silence. Then they began to plan for their people. Before they parted, they decided that the Indians should no longer stay together in one great encampment.

"If we separate," Sitting Bull said, getting wearily to his feet, "it will be harder for the soldiers to find our camps."

"And easier for all of us to find the buffalo," Crazy Horse added, as he knocked the ashes from his pipe. He, too, stood up and soon was riding slowly back to his own village.

The Indians did not scatter at once, however. First, they moved farther north and held a big victory dance. Then, one day, in the Moon When Cherries Turn Black, scouts sent mirror signals that more soldiers were coming, a long way off. And the great camp began to break up. The people tried to be cheerful as they said their good-bys. They talked about meeting again when the whites were gone and the land was at peace. But many of them wondered silently if that day would ever come. It never did.

CHAPTER SEVENTEEN

The End of the Warpath

THE mother of Crazy Horse spoke impatiently. "Look again, Black Shawl, and see if my son is coming."

Reluctantly, Black Shawl put down the spoon with which she was stirring the rabbit stew. For the third time since the sun had left the sky, she went to the entrance of the tepee and peered out into the soft spring night.

"No," she said, choking back a cough, "Crazy Horse still sits alone on the hill."

"Alone," the old woman repeated sadly. "Why must he always be alone? He will not even talk with his father."

"He sits alone," Black Shawl explained, "because he is deciding big things for the people, and he must be by himself to think."

With a little sigh, she turned back to the

fire. Picking up a worn moccasin, she began to patch it with an old piece of deerskin. The moccasin had been made in happier times, many moons earlier, before the big battle with the white chief, Long Hair Custer.

Life had been very hard since that battle. The white men had been furious when they learned that Long Hair and all his men had been killed. Very soon, the White Father had filled the Powder River country with soldiers and told them to hunt the Indians down.

For a while the warriors had been able to hold off the Blue Coats. But at last, Sitting Bull and his Hunkpapas had been forced to flee to the land called Canada. And the Oglalas had been driven from their winter camp on Hanging Woman Creek. After that, many families had hurried south to live on Red Cloud's reservation where they would be safe from white-man guns.

"Yet there are many of us left," thought Black Shawl proudly, as she leaned over to poke up the fire. "Yes, there are many left who will follow my husband wherever he leads."

But where should he lead them? That was the question which Crazy Horse had been trying to settle in his own mind as he sat alone.

[173]

His people were hungry and ragged. They were worn out with fighting. The warriors had no ammunition. The horses were nothing but skin and bones. And the buffalo had been driven away. Again and again the whites had offered food, clothing, blankets, and tents to replace the worn-out tepees if the Sioux would surrender and come in to Red Cloud Reservation.

"If the people are to be saved, there is only one path left for me to take," Crazy Horse told himself. "It leads straight to that jail without walls."

Suddenly he groaned. He hated the white men as bitterly as ever. Could he bear to give up his freedom—to live on white-man land which had once belonged to his own people? Could he bear being watched and ordered about by white soldiers? Truly that would take more courage than fighting.

"You will need courage and strength."

The words seemed to come from far off and Crazy Horse could almost hear his father's voice. In his mind, he was a boy once more, sitting on a hilltop under a starry sky. What else had his father told him that night when they had talked about his vision as they gazed

[*174*]

down at the twinkling campfires of ten thousand happy people?

"A man becomes brave by thinking of others before he thinks of himself," his father had said. "But the way will be hard, my son."

Never before had he dreamed how hard that way would be.

"I would rather be dead than surrender now to the whites," Crazy Horse thought sadly. "For the good of my people I know that I must do it. But I would rather be dead."

He arose and walked slowly down the hill. When he reached the village, he sent a runner to tell the officer in charge of Red Cloud Reservation that the Oglalas were coming in.

So it was that on a cloudless day in May, the Moon of Shedding Ponies, a long procession made its way slowly toward the reservation on White Earth River. Crazy Horse was in the lead, sitting erect on his big white war horse, and wearing a single feather in his hair. Beside him rode Lean Hawk, Big Road, He Dog, and Little Big Man, all with painted faces and feathered war bonnets. Next came the warriors, carrying their lances, shields, bows, and guns. And then the women and children with the travois and pack horses.

[175]

A big crowd of Indians and whites had gathered to watch the Oglalas and to catch a glimpse of their famous war chief. Blue-coated soldiers had been lined up on either side of the road to make sure that there would be no trouble.

Crazy Horse rode by them, looking neither to the right nor left. With lips set tightly together, he led his people past the fort near the reservation, and on to the open space which had been set aside for their village. His eyes blazed with anger, but he said nothing when he was ordered to dismount and his horse was taken away. Then all the horses and all the weapons were given up to the soldiers. It was a hard thing to see and harder still not to make a fight. But the warriors watched their chief and kept the peace as he did.

Before long the women had set up their tepees in a big circle. And the freedom-loving Oglalas tried to settle down to their life on the reservation.

It was not a good life. With little to do and nowhere to go, the people became restless and unhappy. There was quarreling among the warriors. It angered some that others were so quick to take up white-man ways. Little Big Man was one warrior who seemed very eager to please the whites.

Crazy Horse could not understand this change in his boyhood friend. But he had little time to think about it. Though he went often among his people to see that they were well treated, he stayed with Black Shawl as much as possible. For she had caught the white man's coughing sickness. She was growing weaker every day, and Crazy Horse was afraid that she would die.

"Let us go to see my people at Spotted

Tail's reservation," she begged him one day.
"I would feel better if I could talk with them."

"*Hou,*" said Crazy Horse. "We'll go."

Very soon he and Black Shawl were on
their way to Spotted Tail. The news that
Crazy Horse had left Red Cloud spread like
wildfire among the soldiers at the reservation,
and at Fort Robinson, close by. There was
no Indian the white men feared as they feared
this great war chief.

"Crazy Horse has run off!" they told one
another excitedly. "He will persuade the
Brulés at Spotted Tail to join the Oglalas, and
then he will lead them all in a last fight
against us. He must be stopped and brought
back at once."

Immediately, fifty-five Indian scouts who
were friendly to the white men were sent out
to arrest the war chief. Crazy Horse and Black
Shawl had almost reached Spotted Tail when
the scouts overtook and surrounded them.
One of the Indians grabbed at the bridle of
the chief's horse.

"You're running away and you're under arrest!" he shouted.

Crazy Horse drew himself up proudly.

"I am Crazy Horse!" he said quietly. "Don't

touch me. I am not running away. I'm taking my sick wife to her people at Spotted Tail. Let go of that bridle!"

Looking somewhat ashamed, the scout obeyed. Then he and the other Indian soldiers fell back and followed Crazy Horse into the reservation. There the war chief was told

by the officer in charge that he must return to Red Cloud.

"I will go with you to Fort Robinson," said

Major Lee. "And you may tell the soldier-chief just why you left the reservation."

"*Hou*," agreed Crazy Horse with quiet dignity. "I will do that. All that I want now for myself and my people is peace."

The sun was sinking when he and Major Lee and the Indian scouts rode into Fort Robinson. At once Major Lee sent a message to the commanding officer that Crazy Horse had arrived and would like to say a few words to him. But the commanding officer replied that it was too late for a talk that evening. He ordered that Crazy Horse should go with Captain Kennington, who would see that he was given a place to spend the night.

Crazy Horse was tired, and he wished to have no further trouble with the white men. He greeted Captain Kennington and walked with him to a long house which was part of the fort. It seemed strange to the great chief that guards should follow close behind him. And that Little Big Man should be walking so near him, looking far from friendly.

Crazy Horse started to speak with him and then changed his mind. Captain Kennington opened the door of the long house and Crazy Horse stepped inside.

Suddenly he stopped short. Before him were barred cells and men with chains on their legs. So he'd been tricked! They were putting him in prison! In an instant, all his horror of the white-man jails swept over him. With a cry of rage, he swung around, pulling a knife from his belt. Little Big Man grabbed his arm, trying to force him to the ground.

"Let me go! Let me go!" Crazy Horse shouted, fighting his way out into the open.

But now some of the guards seized him. The scouts raised their guns.

"Kill him!" cried one of the officers. "Kill him!"

With his bayonet fixed, a soldier standing behind Crazy Horse lunged forward and stabbed the war chief three times. Slowly the chief crumpled and sank to the ground.

Before the sun walked up the sky next morning, the brave, generous, wise Sioux chief was dead. He had fought courageously for the freedom of his people. And, although that fight was lost, freedom-loving Americans everywhere can remember with pride the great name of a true American—Crazy Horse.

About the Author

ENID LAMONTE MEADOWCROFT was born in New York City but spent most of her childhood in Cranford, New Jersey. There, when she was eleven, she and three school friends started a little newspaper filled with jokes and stories which was hectographed in a backyard shed and sold for five cents a copy. It was then that she first became interested in writing. And she's still interested! THE STORY OF CRAZY HORSE is her nineteenth book for boys and girls. She has lived in nine states, from Maine to Oregon, and has traveled abroad. She now lives in Lakeville, Connecticut, with her husband, Donald Wright. She likes to read, swim, sing, play the piano, work in her garden, and talk with her young neighbors when they drop in after school for cookies and a visit.

About the Artist

WILLIAM REUSSWIG was born in Somerville, New Jersey. He went to school in Utica, New York, and graduated from Amherst College. There, he says, the only prize awarded him was for football, not painting. Since then, his work has appeared in almost all the leading magazines. He took time off along the way to travel in the West, Canada, and Mexico. He went to South America, and to Europe and the Far East as an artist war correspondent in the Second World War. He and his wife, who is also an artist, now live in New Milford, Connecticut. He likes to paint native peoples, historical subjects, and animals, to collect unusual hats and to eat hamburgers.

About the Signature

CRAZY HORSE, as far as we know, never learned to write. No signature of his has ever come to light, and so our artist has stylized his name as the great Indian might have drawn it.

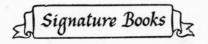

"Names That Made History"

ENID LaMONTE MEADOWCROFT, *Supervising Editor*

THE STORY OF HAYDN
By Helen L. Kaufmann. *Illustrated by John Leone*

THE STORY OF ANDREW JACKSON
By Enid LaMonte Meadowcroft. *Illustrated by David Hendrickson*

THE STORY OF THOMAS JEFFERSON
By Earl Schenck Miers. *Illustrated by Reynold C. Pollak*

THE STORY OF JOAN OF ARC
By Jeannette Covert Nolan. *Illustrated by Pranas Lapé*

THE STORY OF JOHN PAUL JONES
By Iris Vinton. *Illustrated by Edward A. Wilson*

THE STORY OF HELEN KELLER
By Lorena A. Hickok. *Illustrated by Jo Polseno*

THE STORY OF LAFAYETTE
By Hazel Wilson. *Illustrated by Edy Legrand*

THE STORY OF ROBERT E. LEE
By Iris Vinton. *Illustrated by John Alan Maxwell*

THE STORY OF ABRAHAM LINCOLN
By Nina Brown Baker. *Illustrated by Warren Baumgartner*

THE STORY OF MOZART
By Helen L. Kaufmann. *Illustrated by Eric M. Simon*

THE STORY OF FLORENCE NIGHTINGALE
By Margaret Leighton. *Illustrated by Corinne B. Dillon*

THE STORY OF ANNIE OAKLEY
By Edmund Collier. *Illustrated by Leon Gregori*

THE STORY OF LOUIS PASTEUR
By Alida Sims Malkus. *Illustrated by Jo Spier*

THE STORY OF POCAHONTAS
By Shirley Graham. *Illustrated by Mario Cooper*

THE STORY OF MARCO POLO
By Olive Price. *Illustrated by Federico Castellon*

THE STORY OF ELEANOR ROOSEVELT
By Lorena A. Hickok. *Illustrated by William Barss*

THE STORY OF FRANKLIN D. ROOSEVELT
By Lorena A. Hickok. *Illustrated by Leonard Vosburgh*

THE STORY OF THEODORE ROOSEVELT
By Winthrop Neilson. *Illustrated by Edward A. Wilson*

THE STORY OF ROBERT LOUIS STEVENSON
By Joan Howard. *Illustrated by Joe Polseno*

THE STORY OF MARK TWAIN
By Joan Howard. *Illustrated by Donald McKay*

THE STORY OF GEORGE WASHINGTON
By Enid LaMonte Meadowcroft. *Illustrated by Edward A. Wilson*

THE STORY OF MARTHA WASHINGTON
By Jeannette Covert Nolan. *Illustrated by Corinne B. Dillon*

THE STORY OF MAD ANTHONY WAYNE
By Hazel Wilson. *Illustrated by Lawrence Beall Smith*

HANDSOME BOOKPLATES: *Send your name and address to* SIGNATURE BOOKS, GROSSET & DUNLAP, INC., 1107 Broadway, New York 10, N.Y. *We will mail you, on receipt of twenty-five cents to pay postage and handling, a set of forty-five handsomely designed bookplates, each one different.*

1 Born on Rapid Creek, Nebraska, about 1842

2 Goes to Fort Laramie Tre[...] Council, September, 1851

3 Sees Chief Conquering Bear mortally wounded, 1854

4 Goes to great council of Sioux Indians at Bear Butte, 1857

10 Is stabbed by guard at Fort Robinson and dies of wound, September 5th, 1877

9 Surrenders and leads his people to Fort Robinson, May, 1877